Prayer WHEN YOU DON'T Have THE Words

I Walked With Jesus

TAMARA MICHELLE DOBBS

ISBN 978-1-77839-082-1 (paperback)

Copyright © 2024 by Tamara Michelle Dobbs

All rights reserved. No part of this publication may be reproduced, distributed, or transmitted in any form or by any means, including photocopying, recording, or other electronic or mechanical methods without the prior written permission of the publisher.

Printed in the United States of America

CONTENTS

Introduction..9
Preface 11
Acknowledgments..13

Service And Love... 17

Journey To Service..19
Giving Thanks...21
Forgiveness..23
Love Of A Family And Of A Mate 32
Male Or Female Order To God..33
Love's Illusions And Broken Hearts..37
Unrequited Love 41
Truth In A Relationship 42
Marriage...44
Frozen Tears 47

Prosperity, Clarity, Joy, And Peace 49

Prosperity.. 51
Clarity..53
Flow Of Money 56
Depression, Guilt, And Joy In One's Life 60

Children And The Life Cycle..67

Having Children...69
Caregiving And Aging..73
Caregiving 74
Aging..76

Death And Healing 79

Unexpected Passing Of A Child 81
Passing Of A Parent Of A Young Child Or An Adolescent 84
Suicide 86
Prayer For A Person Who Has Taken Their Own Life And
A Prayer For Their Family And Friends 87
Mental Health 90
Grief And Devotion 92
Sisters 94
Devotion And Healing 95
Lost Limbs And Paralysis 97
Someone With A Life Threatening Illness 98
Simple Prayer For A Cure Of A Life Threatening Disease 100
Mercy With Death 101

**Servicemen, Women, And Tyranny Protectors
Of Our Country And Military** 103

Protectors Of Our Country And Military 104
Prisoners Of War And Those Missing In Action 106
Police Men And Women 108
Firemen And Women 110
First Responders And Ems 112
Leaders: Local, State, National, And World 114
Terrorism 116
War And Peace 117
South America And The Children's Crisis 119
Tyranny 121

Addictions, Neighbors, And God 123

Getting Drug Dealers Out Of Your Neighborhood 125
Correct Decision Making 128

Journeys And New Beginnings 133

Moving On 135
Finding A Job And A Place To Live 138
Finding A Home.. 141
Traveling 143
Flying.. 145

Earth And All Our Relations.. 149

Mother Earth... 151
Weather... 154
Cleanup And Integrity 156
Oceans, Lakes, Rivers, Forest, Prairies, And Their Inhabitants 157

Prayers For Yourself.. 161

Prayers For Self 163
Pray Without Ceasing 166

How I Came To Believe 167

I See Angels, And I Walked With Jesus.. 169
The Man In The White Dress: My First Angelic Experience............ 174
Head On With A Mack Truck 177
Angels... 181
Having A Hissy Fit 185
Many Rooms 186
I Walked With Jesus 188

DEDICATION

Prayer When You Don't Have the Words
Is dedicated
To all who are in pain and need hope.

Prayer When You Don't Have the Words is a unique blend of prayer, self-help and a spiritual journey.

INTRODUCTION

Prayer, to me, is as important as breathing, eating, and stretching. The majority of my positive private thoughts are in the form of prayer. The prayers in *Prayer, When You Don't Have the Words* have a story that you may relate to. Most prayers have three parts to them. First, each category contains a story about why the prayer has been written. Second, it has the prayers I wrote for friends and family in need. The third part is in the format of fill-in-the-blank so you may use your own words.

In most of the prayers, I use the term Creator as my greeting. I use this term because I work with so many diverse cultures and religions. Please do not get hung up on this. Pray to God with the terms you are comfortable with. When I am aware of the person's preference on how they address God, I use their words when writing or speaking a prayer for them. I do not judge how you pray, and my request, is that you do not judge me for my tolerance. Please enjoy! This is a book you do not have to read front to back. Find a prayer that touches your heart or need.

The author's story at the end of *Prayer, When You Don't Have the Words* is about a series of events that created the person I am. I believe in Angels, Jesus, and God—all powers greater than I am.

My prayer for you, the reader, is that this book will help you when you cannot find your own words.

PREFACE

Dearest Reader,

This book came together through the request of many people. I have received—and still receive—daily appeals for prayers from people who feel hopeless, or they personally don't have the right words. People tell me their stories, and I ask, "May I pray for you out loud right now?" If the timing is not correct at that moment, I always do a quick, silent prayer. If the timing is off, I wait until I can be somewhere quiet to write a prayer for the person and situation in need. Prayer has always been an integral part of my life. Without the grace of God and prayer, I would not be here. Prayer works!

A while ago, one of my massage clients needed more than a massage. I started the healing session with a vocalized prayer for her situation. This particular lady was so moved.

She asked me, "Why don't you write a book?"

I told her about my Angelic experiences and the book that I have been working on for several years.

Thinking that was awesome, she questioned me, "How about a prayer book?"

I told her I would consider her idea.

A couple of years ago on a cold January day, I received a call from a well-known metaphysical publishing company. The lady that I spoke to stated that she thought I would be a great asset as a speaker for an upcoming convention. My excitement could hardly be contained until I remembered I had a prior commitment. I was curious how she found me. When asked, she stated that she discovered me through my website.

She then asked, "Have you published your book?" I told her the book was still being written. The manuscript would be in an editor's hands by late July.

Until I had spoken those words, the book was just an idea. The journey of the writing and editing is an incredible story of its own. Angel magic in the making!

On a side note, my website was not up when that woman called. I lost the woman's phone number. When I contacted the publisher, I was informed that they do not reach out for potential authors. They told me there are two ways to get published through them. The first is through self-publishing using their link. The other is through the use of an agent. It has been over five years since that first phone call. The pathway to becoming a published author was filled with many hurdles. God's time and my time just seemed to be out of sync until now.

Blessings to you!

ACKNOWLEDGMENTS

Dearest Creator,

I give thanks to You! I give thanks for my Guides and Angels! I give thanks for the family and friends that made publishing *Prayer, When You Don't Have the Words* possible.

I give thanks for my life partner Steven Bray and his parents. I am thankful Steven's parents offered me the opportunity to stay in their home in Michigan for several weeks while I wrote this little book. It only took ten days to write, two years to manifest into a readable form, and five years for it to become the book it was intended to be.

I am thankful that Beth Hagan has been one of my fabulous role models and acted as my first editor. Thank you for being! Peggy RavenWolf, without you, there would still be no book. Thank you for being my friend and a sister of my heart. Charlotte for giving what time you could. Tim Jacobs, I thank you for taking on the task of my final edit of the first printing. I give thanks for Raven Lamoreux-Dodd for helping with my last proofread. I give thanks for John who took my first photographs for the first printing and Jessica for the second set of photographs for the second printing. Special thanks for Michael Braun and his beautiful wife Susan who have made the new cover of *Prayer, When You Don't Have the Words* possible.

I give thanks to those friends and customers who made this journey financially possible.

I give thanks to my mentors from this plane and beyond, for those who know me and those who have yet to meet me. Each one influenced who I am today.

Thank You for all the amazing Earth Angels who have touched my heart with their writings, seminars, and presence.

I give thanks to those who have asked for prayers. (Almost all the names in the prayers have been changed and several have passed on since the writing of this book. I miss you and look forward to seeing you in my dreams or when my time comes to join you.) I give thanks for all those who have prayed for me. The names are not in any order. My apologies if I missed your name. Vivian, Mary, Bryce, Teri, Vicky, Gerald, Marian, Debbie, Patty, Amy, Karen L, Karen M, Karen T, Carol, Mark, Kelly, Kevin, Roger, Mathew, Kim, Bert, Betty, Peggy, Charlotte, Cookie, Dinah, Elise, Eileen, Erin, Maytee, Gracie, Jay, Julie, Kara, Ruth, Larry, Theo, Mike, Louisa, Martha, Rich, Marge, Monique, Nadine, Nelly, Nikala, Beth, James, Pat, Patricia, Sarah, Heather, Raino, Tracy, Abe, Renita, Serena, Phyllis, Timmy, Leslie, Deborah, Kerry, Lisa, Lynnette, Chad, Zac, Ruby, Tricia, Alex, Patty, Jane Francine, Cassie, Angela, Catherine and her staff, Kate and her staff, and my dear friends Neena and Diane who have now left our earthly presence since the beginning of this book. Bill Hernandez, who contributed to this book, two prayers. One prayer on marriage and the other on peace in the middle east. I give thank Lord that you sent Bill to me to help reorganize and add some prayers that were missing in the first edition.

My catalyst of growth. I miss you. Dr. John and Reverend Elamay, without you, my parents and family may have stayed predators and victims. Shelly, you took me on a journey that gave me the power to change my life and speak my truth. Thank you, Mark, for making the journey possible. Aaron T., thank you for the lesson in humility and the importance of integrity and truth. Lori Carlson, you taught me to listen to the little voice. I still listen to your music. Mariana Ray, I listen to your music every day. Without you, I probably would not understand how important forgiveness is and who it really is for. Roseanne, I thank you for being the neighborhood author who never went without asking me about the progress of this book. May your romance novels become bestsellers. You are an incredible writer and one of the best of friends.

I give thanks for Chris and Frances Dobbs, my monsters, my parents. Through them, I learned the good, the bad, and the ugly of human nature. I learned of prayer and meditation; I learned to be strong, they taught me that love conquers everything!

Love Conquers All
To love is to be of service.
Forgiving is to love oneself.
Be thankful for God's Love.

SERVICE AND LOVE

JOURNEY TO SERVICE

I felt that the first prayer in this book should be about my journey. You, the reader, are more than welcome to use it as your own. It is a prayer of commitment! The simple prayer that follows will not be as binding. It is a commitment for service, even if it is a commitment just for today.

Reminder: As stated in the preface, some of the blanks can be used to insert how you address God. The way you address whom you are praying for may be inserted in the other blanks. The ending is how you would end your prayer. Please complete your prayer as you normally would or as you have been trained. Any time "I" is placed in the prayer when "we" would fit better, use what is best.

In most prayers, I give thanks to the Creator, my Guides and Angels, and the Guides and Angels of the person being prayed for. If you are uncomfortable with any title (Creator, Lord, God) or celestial being (Guides, Angels), just omit those words when you read or write your own prayer.

Prayer of Service

Dearest Creator,

I thank You for your presence in my life, for my Guides and Angels. I give thanks for this new day and all the blessings that will come my way. For whatever my service to You brings, whatever You need me to do, I give thanks.

Lord, fill my soul with prisms of light. Help me transform as a caterpillar might. Help my spirit find its way out of the cocoon. My wings are ready. I feel the need to breathe, to fly, to soar.

I ask that my wings be made of titanium and diamonds, uncrushable, unstoppable, and translucent with the strength of angel wings. Creator, I ask that this be the day I come out of my cocoon.

This day and only this day counts. When I wake in the morning, It will be today. And, again, only today counts. I can look to the future and see possibilities. I can look to the past and tap into joys and sorrows; they are not today. Creator, I give thanks for my past as it has given me the strength to do what You ask of me. The past You tempered my wings and made me strong and wise. My past has allowed me to see human suffering, pain, and the lies we tell ourselves. Today allows me to see it is time to reframe the suffering, pain, and lies. It is time for the joy and health of the body, mind, and spirit. It is time to see past the deceit. I choose your path, Lord. Direct me, guide me, and send me those people who are ready. Protect me from those who would attempt to crush me, stop me, or destroy me. I am now committed to You as I have never been before.

I give thanks. So it is!

Simple Prayer of Service

Dearest_____,

I give thanks for your presence in my life, for my Guides and Angels. I give thanks for this new day and all the blessings that will come my way. I ask that I be a servant for the good. I ask that I be given strength, intelligence, courage, and wisdom to follow the path You direct me to walk. I commit my day/life to You,_____. Whatever my service to You brings, whatever You need me to do, I will do what You ask of me.

As Your humble servant, I give thanks.

GIVING THANKS

Just start giving thanks and keep going until you are finished. Keep going until you have run out of things to be grateful for or because you ran out of time while giving thanks. If you do this at least once a day, you will find you are more grateful for what you have. You are more grateful because you became aware of all the blessings you have in your life.

When you first start your prayerful journey, keep a daily journal of something you are grateful for. Sometimes the pain in your life can be so intense, you might find you can only be grateful for your pets/plants or whatever brings you joy or peace. Write a prayer in your journal for them. Learn to be grateful when you stub your toe even though it may seem odd to be grateful for something painful. Be grateful that you only stubbed your toe and did not break it. Think of it as a lesson. Is it a lesson to slow down or to step up? Be grateful for the lessons attached to stubbing your toe. I wanted to give thanks to all the possibilities on the day this prayer was written.

Prayer for Giving Thanks

Dearest Creator,

I give thanks that there is a power greater than I am. I give thanks for the Oneness! I give thanks for where I have been and what I have had to go through to get here. I give thanks for the direction I am now headed. I give thanks for the growth in my life. I give thanks for my mate and his family. I give thanks for my family. I give thanks for my job, the place I work, my coworkers, and customers. I give thanks for my family and friends that have passed before me. I give thanks for my health. My health seems to be getting better every day! I give thanks for my pets that currently live with me and those who have passed. I

Tamara Michelle Dobbs

give thanks for my condo, my car, my loving neighbors, my clothing, air conditioning, plumbing, and money. I give thanks for the lessons in my life. I give thanks for love and that I am loving and compassionate. I give thanks that I am strong. I give thanks for You, the highest power that watches over me, guides me, and protects me.

I give thanks.

Simple Prayer for Giving Thanks

Give thanks for everything you can think of.

Dearest_____,
  I give thanks! So it is!

FORGIVENESS

Forgiveness is an interesting energy. Many people think forgiveness is for the perpetrator of a negative event. Three events changed how I look at forgiveness. Two will be told here. Forgiveness is a journey.

An English woman raised in South Africa, is now an American, a flutist who uses her music in spiritual healings This woman came to Florida in the spring of 1995. She was holding a healing retreat at a local church.

My soon-to-be-husband agreed to go. To this day, I have no remembrance of his healing session. I don't even remember if he had a healing session. I do know; however, I would not be the person I am today without that retreat.

This wonderful woman alternated between playing her flute and talking. She told us to pick the parent with whom we had the most angst with. I chose to work on forgiveness with my father. At the time, I felt I had more issues with him.

I am very visual, so it is easy to glide into self-hypnosis when it is required of me. (I had years of training as a child in transcendental meditation, Sylva Mind Control, and Science of Mind.) Our guide took us on a journey to heal our most difficult relationship. She asked us to see ourselves as children and find something fun that we did with our parents. Time seemed to drag as I could find nothing. Then, in my mind's eye, a snowball hit me fully in the face. Later, my fiancé stated I flinched like I had been hit in the face. His comment made me smile impishly.

I was transported decades back. I saw the snowball fights. I watched us create snow forts while we laughed so hard. Looking at the movie screen in my mind, I relived the water fight which ended up with my father squirting my brother and me with the hose in the living room. I saw how mad my mother was when she discovered water everywhere, including on every piece of furniture. In my mind's eye, I watched the total uncontrolled laughter that rumbled through all four of us. I saw the rubber band fights where we flipped over furniture to use as shields. What I saw almost gave me the giggles. Our guide asked us to forgive the parent we chose. Stubbornly and emphatically, my mind said, "No!"

She had us see our parent as a child during the point where they might have learned their behavior. In a horrible vision, I saw my father at age five. I saw what created his trauma bond and mold how he would eventually see young women.

Our guide asked us to visualize ourselves holding and hugging that child as you would a traumatized child. My heart ached for my father as I began to understand. She asked us to forgive our parent. I found my mind still saying, "No!" What he did had been too awful. His deeds had destroyed too many lives. He had created damaged goods.

The woman then stated, "Forgiveness is not for your parents; it is for you."

Holding on to the anger and rage only hurts you. It does not hurt the parent. My brain mulled that over. She then said some of the most powerful words I ever heard. "If you cannot say I forgive, say I am willing to forgive."

Something in me released all the tension I was holding. All the grief and rage just broke free. I could not forgive, and I was now willing to forgive. A new understanding of my father, and why he was the way he was, had entered my awareness and my heart.

After the retreat, I went home to my parent's condo. I sneaked in. My father was desperate for my attention. Any time I showed up, he would call from his hospital bed or wheelchair. He'd say, "Before you go...before you go...I need you to do..."

I could not step foot into the condo without his beseeching. I resented his demands. I resented his ordering me around. I loved and hated him. Before his stroke, I had asked repeatedly for my mother to divorce my father.

Visiting with my mother was never a peaceful event. Stealthily entering their condo, I held my finger to my lips to keep other family members from announcing my arrival.

My sister was visiting from another state. She asked me how the retreat was.

Smiling, I said, "It was awesome! It was about healing with a parent."

She looked at me quizzically.

Continuing to smile, I fixed two iced teas and went into my dad's room for the first time willingly since his stroke eleven years before.

My father could have been in prison for many reasons. As I sat in his wheelchair and watched this amazing, horrible man sleeping, all I could think of is all the good he had done. I remembered how many times he had stood behind me and defended me when the town bully, the police chief's son, had chosen me as his main target. I remembered how he supposedly never had any money. Dad always found ways for the less fortunate members of our family and neighborhood to have Christmas gifts and food on their tables without letting them know that they came from him. I remember seeing how he changed when we found the Science of Mind Church in a town next to the one we were living in. This scary, abusive, and angry man found his heart. I remember the hours of study that my mother, father, and I put in as a family to become Science of Mind practitioners. If Dr. John had not passed away before my father had finished his fourth year, my father would have been a minister.

Reflecting back, I remembered how the anger started to build again in Dad, especially when we had to take in my grandmother, his mother. I now understood it all. I had his story in my notebook. I had written everything I saw in the vision.

When he woke, I was ready. At first, he was startled after opening his eyes. Then he quickly started to say, "Before you go…"

Smiling, I said, "Dad, I'm not going anywhere. I'm here for a while. After we talk, I'll be glad to give you the time to do any tasks you need acomplished."

I could see relief and confusion in his face. If I could help it, I seldom touched him. I reached out and touched his hand. I looked him squarely in the eyes and said, "Tell me what happened to you when you were five."

He tried to pull away; I continued to hold his hand. I showed him my notebook and said, "I already know. It is all here. I need you to tell me, so we both know that I know." His eyes were like saucers. They filled with tears before he told me everything I already had written down.

I told him I loved him, and that I could not quite forgive him for what he had done to my family. I told him that I knew it was not my place to be his judge and jury, and I was working on forgiving him for my sake.

Jumping back several years, my father had a stroke. He was in a coma for several months. When my father came out of his coma in 1984, he shared a story for the first time. Then, on a spring day in 1995, he told it a second time. Dad told me that he met a panel of twelve souls on the other side, while he was in his coma. The panel of twelve told him that he had made great strides in his lessons, and he couldn't come home until he corrected something that he had made wrong. Dad said that when he fixed whatever it was, he would be forgiven and able to take his rightful place on the other side. The problem was that he did not remember what it was he needed to fix.

He also told me, shortly after he had had his stroke that when I got married, he would be free to go. Unfortunately, I did not put the story and the statement together. In hindsight, I now understand my Father and I had to heal our relationship. If we did, as God expected of us, he then would be able to go home.

For the next six months, I learned to like my father. Instead of tuning him out, I listened for the first time to stories he had been telling for years. During our time together, he apologized for having me use toxic chemicals on the food we grew in the backyard and for having me use muriatic acid in our pool. He had always wanted me to have children, and he felt that part of my problem might have been toxic buildup in my body.

From the stroke he had in 1984, my father had been paralyzed on the right side of his body. During the weekend of my wedding, my Father had a mild heart attack. Fluid had filled his right lung from the heart attack. Dad had no feeling on his right side. He also had no understanding why he felt so weak. My mother and I were normally very in tune with his health issues, and we completely missed the signs of his dis-ease. The heart attack and subsequent pneumonia was not treated.

When I came back from my disastrous honeymoon journey, I received a call from my mother. She asked me to take my father to the hospital. I attempted to brush off their concerns. There were things that my world needed. In addition to my new marriage, I had to get back to work. Both parents persisted in their requests. I took my father later that Monday afternoon.

I remember him asking a nurse, "If I stop eating, how long will it be before I die?"

She stated, "Six days."

It took four. He passed almost three weeks after my wedding.

On the last night before his passing, my father asked me to take my mother home. He was tired and needed to rest.

I did not hug him. I kissed him on the head and said, "Dad, this is not fair. I have respected you, loved you, and adored you. I have also hated your guts. I've finally come to peace, even learning to like you, and now you are leaving."

Dad said truthfully, "I taught you at the age of four that life was not fair."

I knew without a doubt that he was dying. In my mind, I had two more days to see him, hug him, and remind him that he was loved. The hospital called us in the middle of the night on October 17, 1996 to tell us that my father passed. I had no idea how painful it was going to be. I didn't know how much I would miss him. I didn't realize how many times I would pick up the phone and call to bounce something off him, just to hear my mother say, "You forgot again, didn't you?" We would both cry.

My beliefs about death are different than most. I have been to the other side a few times. I have no fear of death, and yet I mourn with intensity. That is something about myself I do not quite understand. I have created a statement. I call death the "Un- Huggables and the Address Unknown." There is no place on the planet where I can go to hug the person that has crossed over. In my mind's eye, I hug you, Papa. For now, it's the best I can do!

A Prayer for my Saints and Sinners Chris and Fran Dobbs:

Prayer of Forgiveness

Dearest Creator,

I give thanks for You and my Guides and Angels. Creator, I give thanks, for my father and my mother. I know, Creator, I was put into this family to learn, to grow, and to be chiseled like a diamond. Living and growing with these people who were like Greek heroes has not been easy. Both were larger than life and beautiful. They were full of love, passion, and anger. And they were confused. They lead with their hearts, unless their addictions ruled. As my mother said one day, "I apologize for not raising you the way you thought you should be raised, and I will not apologize for living my life with the wisdom and knowledge I had at the time."

Creator, I give thanks that I was given that apology and the apology my father gave me before he died. I give thanks that some part of me is still innocent and tempered with wisdom.

I ask God that You help me totally forgive my mother and father. Help me understand that they did the best they could with the tools they had. Help me go beyond being willing to forgive. I give thanks that Fran and Chris were my parents and that they gave me the strength to overcome and love unconditionally.

Thank You!

Forgiveness Continued

I had attended a course called "Understanding Yourself and Others," also known as UYO in December of 1998. (If these programs are still running somewhere, I highly recommend allowing yourself the privilege of letting go of some major hurts in a safe environment.) Many very painful memories came up during that course. A realization came to me that there were as many issues with my mother as there had been with my father. My mother and I were roommates at the time. My marriage was ending and Dad had been gone a little over two years. The discovery I made about the relationship with my mother disturbed me, and it also set something in me free. She protected me and did not protect the others girls in my family from my father. She had used me to control my dad. She used me as a weapon. After experiencing the UYO event, I asked her for an apology for staying with my father. My mother was highly offended at the time.

Out of the blue, three months later, she cornered me in the bathroom while we were getting ready to attend a funeral. I was putting on makeup. Standing behind me, she faced me in the mirror and stated, "I have thought long and hard about what you asked of me."

She looked so serious. I thought, "Oh, crap! What did I ask of her?" My second unvoiced thought was, "We're okay right now, I think?"

I said, "What did I ask of you and when did I ask it?"

She responded, "You asked me for an apology before Christmas. I apologize for not raising you in the manner you believe you should have been raised. I will not apologize for living my life with the wisdom and knowledge I had at the time. It was my life! I had my own lessons to learn."

I remember telling her that some of those lessons were excruciatingly painful and were not my lessons. She thanked me for helping her transcend some of those painful lessons. She was my "Momster," and I loved her with all my heart.

A couple of weeks after my mother had given me her apology, I attended a Sunday service at a local church in Florida. The subject of the sermon was forgiveness. The minister was an awesome teacher and mentor. He filled his church, even out of season. Everyone loved him. He began his sermon by asking a question of the congregation.

"Why are we here on this planet?" The congregation responded. Several stated, "To love, to teach, to help."

I stood up and said clearly, "To learn!"

The minister pointed at me and said, "Correct!"

I sat down, amazed at myself for being so bold.

He went on to say forgiveness is not for others, it is for us. He asked his audience, "What is the best way to learn?"

After several people had yelled out reasonable answers, I stood up and said, "By making mistakes."

Part of my brain was very happy that I had not brought anyone with me. I had properly embarrassed myself. I had the answers he was asking, and it irritated me that I had put myself out there. I was irritated only for a few moments. Then I began listening and learning.

The minister questioned, "If we are here to learn...and the best way is to make mistakes...if we make mistakes, aren't we performing what we came to this planet for?"

"Holy crap!" I thought. "I just had my brain scrambled."

He went on to say, "If we are here to make mistakes, then there really is nothing to forgive."

"Now my brain is in the blender on purée!" I thought to myself as a light bulb went off in my head. The people who had hurt my family and friends, people who had betrayed me or thought I had betrayed them, were all misguided. Each of us was busy learning our lessons. My dad was the way he was because of his lessons, my mother the same way. I was to learn from them and transcend. My need to forgive and be forgiven was actually a path for love and peace. I wholeheartedly believe this. I started using the minister's paraphrased words in my healing sessions. Miracles started happening with my clients.

I still needed to use the word "forgiveness" in my work. Most people felt shame for things that had been done to them or for things they had done to others. I created a forgiveness prayer to be used in my healing sessions.

Prayer of Forgiveness

Dearest Creator,

I give thanks for You and my Guides and Angels. I give thanks for the opportunity to share this time with Cyndi. We ask, Creator, that this be a healing session. Cyndi has come to me with anger in her heart. She feels as if her soul has been wounded and wants to let it go. Creator, we ask that You help her understand that she is here to learn lessons, lessons about appropriate boundaries, about love for others, and about self-love. As in the Lord's Prayer, forgive us our trespasses as we forgive those who trespass against us. We ask, Creator, that the forgiveness reach Cyndi's heart. We ask that forgiving, helps Cyndi to heal body, mind, spirit, and soul!

We give thanks! So it is!

Simple Prayer for Forgiveness

Dearest_____,

I give thanks for your presence in my life. I need help forgiving myself and_____. The forgiveness I need for myself is because I have held onto anger and resentment. I need to let go of these intense negative feelings and move forward. I am willing to forgive_____ and turn this situation and this relationship over to You. I ask for peace of mind, love, and joy in my life, and I give thanks that you are here to help fill my heart with only Love.

God Bless!

LOVE OF A FAMILY AND OF A MATE

This prayer was written in the fall of 2000. My life partner and I had crossed paths several times since 1979; never once did he make a solid impression. Within weeks of writing this prayer, I was officially introduced to the man who was to become my life partner. The man embarrassed me in such a way; there was no way to ignore him as I had several times in the past. I love him to distraction. Words of caution when you use this prayer: make sure you know what you want and that you are ready for it. The prayer was written as a positive affirmation. Even so, it is pure prayer. This one pretty much covers the simplified prayer.

Prayer for Love

Lord,

Love surrounds me; it permeates my soul. I give and receive only love. My earth walk is all about love and joy. I touch many lives with the love and joy that I am!

I am open to receiving love and joy from others. I accept this now!

I am open to receiving love and joy from my primary relationships: my mother, brothers, sisters, and their spouses. I accept this now!

I am open to receiving love and joy from my nieces and nephews. I accept this now!

I am open to receiving love from my aunts, uncles, and cousins. I accept this now!

I am open to receiving love and joy from a mate. I am open to accepting a mate in my life who treats me with love, honor, respect, compassion, and as an equal. I accept the right loving person, now! I give thanks to You for love, and I accept that love now!

MALE OR FEMALE ORDER TO GOD

When I wrote this prayer, I had to be very honest with myself. I don't like to think of myself as shallow. I had to know what appeals to me, what I did not like, what I would tolerate, and what my needs were and are. The key to this prayer is to have fun with it. Be very specific and watch who God sends to you.

I have a tendency to like darker-skinned, darker-haired men with dark eyes. Italians, Native American Indians, Asians, or and not limited to Lebanese. I have dreamt of a dark-haired, dark-eyed, olive-skinned man since I was seven. My mate is Italian and Native American. Don't get me wrong, I love to look at an attractive, light- eyed blond or a well-groomed, bald man. A relationship with less than full attraction, however, just would not have worked for any great length of time. If Mr. Right had turned out to be the latter, my eyes would have wandered back to the type that I have always been fascinated by. Considering my mate waited almost 15 years for me to finally pay attention to him, not knowing what I wanted in a mate may have caused me to never open my eyes and heart to recognize that he was in front of me.

If you have a thing about breath, teeth, hair, nails, feet, or body odor, make sure you state it in your prayer! The comment in the following prayer that requests my new mate have his own hair and teeth was added to my original prayer after a particularly disturbing and funny first and last date. The date was a definite "Eww! experience."

Money. Be absolutely clear about what you want his money situation to be. If you have a lot of money, and it's not an issue, don't worry about this one. Make sure you mention in your prayer that your new mate has integrity. Oh and sex! You must state in your request for a mate that he or she likes sex as much or as little as you do. If you like a lot of sex, your mate must be capable of meeting your needs.

I wrote this prayer like a child asking to go to Disney and imagining all I wanted to do and see when I got there. I barely took the time to breathe before my next request was made. So if it seems a bit scattered and in your face, it is.

Male Order to God, Prayer

Dearest Creator,

I have reached the time in my life that I would like a life partner. I'm putting in my "Male-order," and I pray You send him to me. Here is my list. If, when I'm finished with my list, You have someone better in mind for me, please send him.

Creator, I have some physical requests. First I'll state the more important requests.

I'll start with qualities that I need in a mate. He must be kind, loving, and funny. He must have an awesome sense of humor. This is particularly important! He gets my humor and I totally get his. He finds me sexy at whatever weight I am. I find him sexy at whatever weight he is. He must be healthy in body, mind, spirit, and soul.

My family must be able to accept him and hopefully love him. And he must be able to accept them and hopefully love them. His family must accept and love me. I must accept and love them.

He must like sex! He must be healthy-minded about sex. He must love children appropriately. He must be excited if it turns out that I can have a child and not be too disappointed if I cannot.

This man must have his own money and not depend on mine. He needs to graciously receive what I give him and share in paying the bills. He must be generous with his time and money, especially to me! He must have some sort of legal income. Money must positively flow in our relationship. It is essential that finances not be something that we will argue about.

This man and his friends must have integrity. I must like his friends and they must be respectful to me. He must accept and even like my friends and always be appropriate with them. He must be trustworthy and must trust me. I would like him to be able to dance, sing, and play a musical instrument. Any or all of these talents would be awesome.

I would like him to be like-minded; if not like-minded, he should be open-minded to the possibilities of being like-minded. I would like us to be equally intelligent. I would like him to see me as an equal, a partner, a person whom he respects. I want to be someone he would like to spend the rest of his life with, someone he calls his friend. I need him to be available emotionally as well as physically. Divorced or widowed is fine as long as he has healed from the experience.

He has to have had some addictions he has worked through; otherwise, he would just be too perfect. I would like him to have worked through his addictions.

If he comes into my life with children, I pray that they grow to love and respect me. If he has an ex-wife, I ask that she be happy in her current relationship and give us her blessing.

Now for the shallow things: I ask that he be dark-eyed, slightly darker-skinned than I am, and I prefer that he have his own hair and teeth. I would like him to be well-groomed with nice hands and a good scent. I would also like him to know how to cook. I would like him to want an orderly home, but please don't send me a neat freak or a slob.

Creator, I leave this prayer open to add as needed if there is anything I left out. I give thanks that You have my Angels working on this even before I end this prayer.

So it is.

Side note here: After I had been with my mate for about two years, I realized one of my requests was not specific enough. I pulled out my original prayer and added to it. The situation was so bad that I was willing to walk away if the new wrinkle was not fixed. I physically rewrote the prayer with the addendum. Within one week, the issue I prayed about started to correct itself. Thank you, God!

Tamara Michelle Dobbs

Simple Prayer for a Male/Female Order to God

I think you, the reader, may get the gist of this one. Just go for it! Be specific! Blessings to you in your endeavor! May you get the mate of your best dreams!

LOVE'S ILLUSIONS AND BROKEN HEARTS

I wrote this prayer for a friend of a very close friend, Cheryl. She found the love of her life. Morton had it all. He was retired and three years older than she was. He was an excellent musician and wrote a song about her. (What woman doesn't want a song about her?) He was slightly taller than Cheryl. He was sexy, intelligent, and seemed kind. He was divorced with six children by two different wives. He owned property and had, according to him, enough money for her and her two twin daughters to move in. He requested that my friend not work. He asked that she help him with household duties and become his muse.

Cheryl and her estranged husband, Bill, were still married. This couple was in the middle of a divorce when he found out he had cancer. He loved his daughters. With his illness, he decided not to divorce Cheryl. Instead, Bill moved back to his hometown thousands of miles away. Cheryl and her husband were divorced in every way except for the paperwork. He loved Cheryl enough to make sure Cheryl and the twins would benefit when he died. Bill could not live with Cheryl. The relationship was toxic to both of them. They had been separated for over 3 years when Morton came into Cheryl's life.

Cheryl seldom dated; she put all her energy into raising her daughters and making sure the food was on the table and a roof was over their heads. She had an excellent job. When Morton offered to take care of her and her daughters, Cheryl bought the new man's fairy tale lock, stock, and barrel.

Within weeks of moving in with him, she could see some red flags. There were many indications that things were not how Morton originally presented them. Cheryl, wanting to be loved so much, was unwilling to see the truth. They did whatever he wanted to do. Plans that were discussed before she moved in (her dreams) were dropped for "more important issues." She became convinced that her interests were his interests, so it did not matter that things previously important to her were no longer of importance.

She learned that five of Morton's children had been or were addicts. Cheryl started hearing complaints from Morton's lifelong friends that he would all of a sudden go cold on them. She started seeing him be friendly and apparently warm toward one person, and the next day he refused to have anything to do with that person. Morton convinced Cheryl that it was important to remove the friend from their lives because of some slight or action the friend took.

She thought she was safe. Morton made love to her daily, sometimes more. He told her that until she came into his life, there was never anyone who made him happier. She was his muse, his love. Less than two years into the relationship, the sex slowed down. He seemed withdrawn and blamed it on his first and second families. There were legalities that had to be taken care of. Morton borrowed money from her to pay for attorneys. He had a lot of money. Why was he borrowing from her? He said he was stressed, so that was why he sometimes slept in the basement. He did not want to disturb her while he tossed and turned. Cheryl helped him with the legalities and saved him over a million dollars. Morton asked her to move out in April of that year. He then recanted. He begged her to stay and forgive him. Everything was good for a few months.

In the fourteen months of their relationship, Cheryl's first husband Bill moved back to be close to his daughters because he was dying. Bill decided he needed to meet Morton. The two men immediately liked each other; they got along very well.

Twenty months into the dream relationship between Cheryl and Morton, it became a nightmare. Bill died. Exactly one day after Bill's death, Morton, who two weeks before said he could not live without Cheryl because she was the love of his life, kicked Cheryl and the twins out. She had the children to think about and needed to find a place close to the school. Cheryl asked that Morton give her time to find a new place to live close to the grade school they attended. He agreed, but stated if she did not have daughters, he would want her out of his house immediately. Cheryl was devastated. She had grieving children to deal with, regrets and grief from the first marriage with Bill to deal with, and now the one who should have had her back pulled the rug right out from under her.

I wrote this prayer for her using words that she spoke to me. I wrote it as if she might have written it.

Prayer for Cheryl, Love's Illusions and Broken Hearts

Dear God,

My heart is broken. I thought Morton was to be the one, my soul mate. What I saw, what I wanted to see, was so perfect. He treated me with kindness. He seemed to see into my soul and understand what I needed and wanted. I became like a sponge, loving every minute. He was the mate I have always dreamed of. And now it is all gone!

I have no understanding. Yesterday I was the love of his life, and today he will not return my calls. My friends and family tell me it is for my best and highest good. What do they know? Those people who are hovering have said, "We have tried to tell you." I ask that You have those well-meaning people leave me alone. God, all I want is Morton. If I cannot have him, I ask for clear answers as to why I cannot have a life with this person. Where did it go wrong? What flags did I miss? Will I ever be able to trust again? Will I be alone?

God, please help me fill my heart with peace and understanding. Help me be open to receiving love again; help my heart to heal. I ask that I not live my life alone. I beseech, You, Creator, for a loving, honest, mentally, physically, and financially well off partner. I request a person who is something like Morton, and more of the real thing.

I give thanks that through You all is possible.

Tamara Michelle Dobbs

Simple Prayer for Love's Illusions and Broken Hearts

My heart is broken. I thought he/she was to be the one, my soul mate. What I saw, what I wanted to see was so perfect. He/she treated me with kindness; he/she seemed to see into my soul and understand what I needed and wanted. I became like a sponge, loving every minute. He/she was the mate I have always dreamt of. Now the dream is all gone. I have no understanding. Yesterday I was the love of his/her life, and today_____ will not return my calls.

My friends and family tell me it is for my best and highest good. What do they know? These people who are hovering have said, "We have tried to tell you." I ask that You have them leave me alone. All I want is_____. If I cannot have him/her, I ask for clear answers as to why I cannot have a life with this person. Please help me to have peace of mind. Please help me find love again. Please help me believe that a loving, honest relationship is possible. I ask that You help my heart to heal.

I give thanks that through You all is possible.

So it is!

UNREQUITED LOVE

As I was finishing my last prayers for this book, I received a phone call from someone who wanted my help with her teenage daughter. The daughter was obsessing about a man who would not give her the time of day. Her mother explained, "She's pining away, and I am worried she will do something dramatic and stupid."

I remembered when I had such a crush on a young man named Dan. Even as I matured, I knew that if I ran stark naked in front of this young man, he just did not have the eyes to see me. I am still unsure why chemistry is sometimes one sided. It was one sided forty years ago, and unfortunately for this young woman it's one sided now. This prayer will be written in the simplistic form for all unrequited loves.

Simple Prayer for Unrequited Love

Dearest _____,

I feel so forlorn, so lost and empty. I love _____ and he/she doesn't even know I am on this planet. I ask, _____, that You open his/her eyes to see my beauty and my worth. I ask if it is not possible to open his/her eyes that You open my eyes to see them in a true light. I ask _____ that You send me someone that I find as exciting or as endearing who also sees me. I ask that somehow, some way, You send me requited love.

I give thanks that in your name all is possible.

TRUTH IN A RELATIONSHIP

A friend of mine had the sneakiest husband. He couldn't tell the truth if his wife's life depended on it, and when he did tell the truth no one believed him. She loved this man with all her heart.

One day in a healing session, I heard in my head, "Tell Jane to ask her husband about the money and the woman." Jane was intuitive and blurted out, "You're supposed to tell me something."

Well, crap! Everything went downhill from there. Jane had on blinders as far as her husband was concerned. This is the prayer for truth I wrote for her.

Prayer for Truth in a Relationship

Dear Father, Mother, God,

I give thanks for your Being! I give thanks for life that encompasses all that I interact with directly or indirectly. May this prayer letter be for all, and may it focus at this moment for my friend Jane and her family situation.

I pray for the truth, that all secrets will be exposed and right action will take place from the exposure of the secrets. I ask that the appearance of great loss be only an illusion to facilitate Jane and her family in learning their lessons. I ask for clarity of thought for Jane. With this clarity, she will be able to act accordingly with confidence, love, and a positive attitude.

I pray when these lessons are over, Jane will be able to look back and see the right action taking place in her life. I ask that she get an understanding why everything had to happen just the way it did. I ask that my friend be given the strength and courage to do what is expected and needed of her. I ask that Jane have peace of mind. I ask that she recognizes love in all its forms. As Jane's human condition unfolds, I ask that she find at least two moments of joy for every moment she is out of balance. I give thanks, Creator, for sending Jane to me and for allowing me as your servant to make a positive difference. May You and your Angels answer the prayers Jane requests that are for her greatest and highest good.

So it is!

Simple Prayer for Truth

Dearest_____,

Something is not right here. I cannot figure it out. Something is hidden, and I feel as if I am the last to know. I ask, whatever I am not seeing, whatever I am not understanding that the truth be shown to me. I am afraid of the unknown. I ask for the truth, and I ask if at all possible the truth be shown to me gently. I ask when the secrets are out, that I will not feel like a fool. I pray the truth is found out in time to protect my heart, my assets, and my life. I give thanks for You and my Guardian Angels. I give thanks for your protection.

So it is!

MARRIAGE

My personal experiences with marriage have not been the best. I left this out in the first printings of this little book. Almost everyone I know has been at least divorced once, including myself. I have one friend who married her childhood sweetheart and forty years later is still married. I asked her how have you stayed married. Here are her rules.

1. Laugh, whatever the issue, find the ridiculousness of the situation.
2. Listen to each other and if you have children listen to them.
3. If you have children make sure you are on the same page with allowances, rewards, rules and discipline.
4. Never correct your mate in front of others.
5. Do not argue in front of the children or other family members.
6. Think twice about appearances. If someone comes up and kisses your spouse do not assume your mate initiated or reciprocated. DO NOT ASSUME THE WORSE!
7. Recognize you may have different love languages. Figure their love languages are and honor them. Share with your spouse your love language.
8. Be clear in your communication.

Another friend asked if he could share his prayer for marriage. Bill Hernandez's contribution will follow the prayer I wrote. I wrote mine before I read his contribution. Bill's prayer says it all.

Marriage Prayers.

Dear Lord,

Marriage between two people would seem to be a joyous and easy proposition. I have found it is a lot of work and not always fun, joyous or even comprehensible. I ask of You, God, to help us to find our humor, joy and tolerance,not take every little disagreement to heart. I ask that You help our love and bond to strengthen over the years and You help us be on the same page with money, children, family, friends, spiritual beliefs and where we want to live. Help us watch over each other and keep us safe from those who would damage our marriage. We give thanks for your protection and love. So it is.!

Prayer for Marriage:

Author: Bill Hernandez

Dear God,

Thank you for the gift of marriage and for being the source of love. We come before you today, asking for a stronger bond of unity in our marriage covenant. Help us to remain content and in love with one another for all our days to come. We want a marriage that reflects Your kind of commitment, Lord. We pray for better communication in our marriage, so that we may understand each other and prevent misunderstandings. We also pray for joy in our marriage, to remain joyful in all circumstances and in each other's presence. Lord, we ask that you strengthen our bonds and our relationship. Bless our marriage and remove anyone who is an obstruction to our union. Instill within us that loving peace, love, and harmony towards each other, that only you can give. May we grow together in faith, trusting you oh Lord. We stand strong on Your Word which has given our relationship a firm foundation, based on faith and truth. With You at the center of our relationship, there is no fear that we will be fruitful and prosperous in everything we do and faithful to each other. May our union be known by Your love. We pray that our actions toward each other would reflect Your character. May our devotion in marriage be a radiant reflection of your love for us. May our marriage always bring glory to You, joy to one another, and blessings to our family for many generations to come. May love and laughter fill our hearts and our home for all the days of our lives. May we face every challenge hand-in-hand and side-by-side knowing that with Your grace, we'll conquer all obstacles together. May the world be forever a better place because we fell in love. We ask all of these in Your name, Amen.

FROZEN TEARS

By Frances Dobbs 1921 -2013

Snow could be the frozen tears of angels,
Falling from the sky.
It may be my consolations,
Knowing they too cry.
Yes, its soft cool beauty,
Dulls the pain and warms my heart...
Takes the bitterness and hate of living,
Stop my tears, and then I start.
Dreaming, dreaming, dreaming,
Smiling, almost laughing, then I sigh;
Dreaming brings remembering...
Memories bring together you and I.
The sifting snowflake is a curtain,
Through its lacy pattern shows a sky, pale blue;
With this peaceful blue and whiteness,
Slowly, dimly, come to life a dream of you.
Together we go back to when the dream was real,
Of love and you and I.
And memory brings me every dream we knew,
Down to the nightmare of good-bye,
Pale blue blends with evening,
Dreams are ending, this I know.
Dazedly I reach to touch you, hold you close before you go.
Broken dreams like bubbles, all is gone;
I am alone and night is near,
Tears like snowflakes silently falling;
Soon they'll stop... reality is here.

If your hands are closed in a fist, how can you be open to receiving God's gifts?

PROSPERITY, CLARITY, JOY, AND PEACE

PROSPERITY

Prosperity is one of the things that we, as humans, limit. We limit what prosperity means. Many of us think of prosperity and wealth only in terms of money, and then we think of it as finite. The richest (money) men and women in the world look at money as if it is air. It's just there to be used. The "normal" person looks at money as if it's the last tasty cookie. It must be either eaten right away and meagerly shared with everyone they feel is worthy or hoarded because there might not be any more cookies. Until writing this, I never looked at money like air. I paused typing just to take in several deep breaths.

As a side note, when I decided to write *Prayer When You Don't Have the Words*, I started squirreling away my tips from my massage practice. I hoarded every penny I could. I figured out it would take me ten days to type the book (really?) and four days to travel and put together the materials for two other books that are basically written. I needed enough put aside to pay all my bills for a month. I started looking for a place to write. The requirements were the following: mountainous with waterfalls, secluded, not too secluded, and preferably free or within my budget. What happened was much different from expected. Here is the first prayer I wrote for that journey. Notice the limitations I put on myself in the prayer. Nothing was expounded on, and it was a beginning.

Prayer for Prosperity

Dearest God,

I dreamt last night that I was to write several books. The first book was to be on and about prayer. I was asked to put my needs into writing to ask You for what I might need. At first, Creator, I thought, "Well, God knows what I need. Why do I need to ask when the answer is already known?" I heard in my head, "So you will believe and you will know!"

Creator, my requirements are simple. I request a peaceful place. I need a place to relax and write. This place must be away from work, my mate, and the daily stress of making a dollar. I need a place where I can take a working computer, all my journals, notepads, and research. I must be able to sprawl these journals out, so I can tear them apart and reorganize all the material for the next two books. The place must be affordable. If I need to sell some of my inherited items, I request help from the Angels to accomplish that task.

I give thanks for the answers as You provide them.

CLARITY

Not much definition in the prayer. I asked for help from the Angels, then I immediately made myself responsible for creating the money to make the trip. I also squashed travel and organizational and creative time to zero. Really? Ten days, fourteen with travel?

I was offered a cabin for free. The offer sounded great at first. I was so excited that I stopped looking for a place to stay, then I discovered there were tentacles attached to the offer. The hunt for an appropriate place to write began again. Many places might have fit my needs, all were too expensive. I don't just mean money! Sometimes free is much more costly than paying a cash price.

I started telling people about the journey and the books that wanted to be written, not the book I had been telling people about for years. I was talking about a new one, one based on something people requested of me every day. I was going to write a book on prayer, filled with prayers and lessons.

In January, I had a call from a woman who asked me if I would be interested in speaking at a convention in Fort Lauderdale, Florida. She had found my website and felt I would be a good fit.

Doreen Virtue would also speak at this convention. OMG! I was so excited. Doreen is part of my story. To meet her again and even be on the same itinerary was such a dream of mine. Reality struck. I sadly told the lady, "I am not ready."

She asked me, "Have you finished your book?"

That comment and the rest of the conversation would cause me to reflect.

I said, "No, I'll be working on it the last couple of weeks in June. It will be ready for an editor by the last week of July."

As those words came out of my mouth, I realized the words were being heard for the first time by anyone, including myself.

She said, "If your book is in the editor's hands by the end of July, give me a call. I would love to have you on the next program happening in the early winter in New York."

"I'll be in touch."

After I hung up, I reflected on the conversation. This woman had said she had found my website. My website was down. She asked me if my book was finished. How did she know I was writing a book? Why did I say late June, early July? Normally, I am busy until late July in my massage practice. My business drops off completely in August and September. Typically, I have ten regular customers every week, and the rest of the week fills in with people I meet at networking events or who find out about me through business associates and friends. Typically, I work on thirty to forty people in a fifteen-day cycle.

My schedule was almost completely clear from June 19 to July 21. The clearing was a little too early and went too long. I started to freak. I had only four massages on my books for the next fifteen days and only ten over the next month. A whole month! How could I afford to go, to be away from work that long?

I did not see it as an opportunity. I totally went into fear mode.

"Oh no!" I thought. "I have to figure this out. I have to sell something and sell it now!"

I went into "squirrely" mode. I spent hours on the computer learning how to put items on EBay. I entered all my information. If I just sold three of my inherited stamps, all my financial problems would just go away. Then all the money I had been hoarding just went POOF! I had access to $87 plus two paychecks that were weeks away. The stamps that I was going to sell did not sell. The place that was being lent to me was too close to home, without woods, without mountains, and without waterfalls. Work was ten miles away, and my mate and his whirlwind activities were basically in the backyard. I burst into tears. Here are my prayers and what happened when I stopped to listen to the answers.

Prayer for Clarity of an Issue

God,

I don't understand! I know with my whole being that I am to write this book. I dream about it, think about it, and talk about it all the time. I am consumed with writing this book. You are sending me people who need prayers, desperate people who just don't have the words. Why am I being thwarted? Why am I being blocked? I need help!

I turn this problem over to You!

Simple Clarity Prayer

One thing about a clarity prayer is that you need to write or say exactly what you think the problem is. Be as specific as possible.

Dearest _____,

I am confused. I am praying for clarity on this issue_____. I am asking for direction and the correct action I should be doing or saying. I ask for clarity and guidance. I trust in You and know You will guide my way. I give thanks for your presence in my life!

So it is!

FLOW OF MONEY

Within an hour, a girlfriend called. She said, "Tamara, how's the plans to get yourself up here in North Carolina?" Tears falling, I shared with her how everything I had attempted to put together fell apart, except for the time off. I told her about how the time had actually opened up. I was worried about day-to-day bills. I also told her about the prayer and how the situation had been turned over to God.

She insisted, "Tamara, now really turn it over to God. We know you're supposed to do this project. You are supposed to be in the mountains."

I reiterated that prayers had been made. At that point, I just could not see how it was going to work out. On the same day, June 16, I had four massages on my schedule for the next fifteen days. I just completed work on one of the four massages when my phone rang. My friend William's name came across the caller ID. I smiled with joy, and the smile registered in my voice across the phone. William was one of many whom I had helped facilitate his waking up to his abilities as a healer and a Shaman. William and I connect maybe three times a year, usually not to help each other. We connect to ask for help for other people. He asked me what was going on in my life. I laughed. William said my laughter had a lot of pain hiding in it. I shared with him what was going on.

After a few minutes, William said, "Tam, I don't have a lot of money, but the moment you say you are hitting the road, I will wire you $200 for gas. You're going, you know!"

The moment I got off the phone, I knew the local condo I was to stay in was no longer going to be available. I needed to talk to my mate's family. They were my family! It would work. Feeling inspired, I sent out a request to friends and customers who had become friends to come in and get massages or Reiki sessions. A request was put out to some friends who had the ability to help if they would buy packages of home sessions from me. I told every one of them why I was in need of gathering money. $2,500 was the golden number that I needed beyond what I had coming in at that moment.

That night, I was told the local home was going on the market, so staying there was no longer an option. (That home is actually in one of the prayers in this book.) My intuition had already prepared me for that news, so I was not devastated by the apparent loss of a sanctuary to write in. My mate and his parents brainstormed as a family.

Pops suggested to me, "How about the home in Wisconsin? No one will be there for almost three weeks. It's empty. Your requirements would be met. There are even waterfalls and rapids in the area."

My first limited thought and response was, "That is a long way to drive."

Pops asked, "How important is it?

I said, "I can leave next Tuesday."

My mate said, "Make sure your bills are covered here."

Whew! No pressure there.

Prayer for Flow of Money

Dearest Creator,

I give thanks for You, Creator, for my Guides and Angels. I give thanks for the wealth that I have. I give thanks for being your servant, Creator. I have so many people in my life that love and honor me. I am so blessed. As in the poem "Desiderata," I know I am no less than the trees and the stars. The countless blades of grass and sand on the beaches should teach me that there is more than enough. Money is energy. Like the tide, money comes in and goes out. I cannot stop the tide nor do I want to. Why do I stop the flow of money in my life? Through You, I know I can and will learn to harness the energy of money. I know in the past that I have limited my belief. I have made statements. "There is never enough." "If I had more, I would give more." "Money doesn't grow on trees." "I would love to, and I can't afford the cost." These limiting statements have kept me from accepting the many gifts from You.

I release these limiting beliefs. From this day forward, Creator, I am changing my thoughts, my words, and my actions. I ask, Creator, that You help me strengthen my belief in abundance. I accept an abundance of time, money, energy, and love. My life through my trust and belief in You fills my soul. I am overwhelmed with joy. Through You, everything is possible. All my needs are met and exceeded.

So it is in Christ's name!

The prayer above not only mentions money; it covers time, money, energy, and love. Prosperity is all the above. Prosperity flows better when we are grateful for what we have.

Simple Prosperity Prayer

Dearest,

I give thanks for this blessed day; I give thanks for You, for my family, and my friends. I give thanks for the roof over my head, food in my belly, and that I live in a country where I have the freedom to change my prosperity levels. Statements made by people in my past and the struggles that I watched my family go through have left me with the fear that there will never be enough. I need to be without the fear of wondering if I will have enough to pay my rent and pay for groceries. I need to fret less and be able to focus more on the important things in life.

I am devoted to my belief in You. I know that through You all things are possible. I ask that you open my eyes to new ideas that bring in a healthier financial lifestyle. I am not a greedy person. I understand that with better cash flow, I can be a more generous person. I may help myself, my family, my friends, my community, my country,

and my planet.

I believe I would be a good custodian and use a positive cash flow wisely. I ask for a divine idea or a gentle nudge to open my heart to financial freedom and all the positive responsibilities that go with that new freedom. I give thanks and accept this new way of thinking and living. I give thanks!

DEPRESSION, GUILT, AND JOY IN ONE'S LIFE

There was a very dark time in my life. I was healing from a debilitating back and neck injury. I had just become a Reiki practitioner and licensed massage therapist. I opened my own business and got married to a man that I had known for several years. Within three weeks of getting married, my handicapped father had a heart attack and died. Over the next few months, the promise and hope I felt disintegrated. I lost my hope and had new responsibilities, some of which I had expected and many new burdens that were not expected.

I felt like Job in the Bible. My first affliction was kidney stones. Louise Hay in her book, *You Can Heal Your Life*, would say "unshed tears." I had no time for tears. Our second problem was that my husband was sick. We thought he had cancer.

His stepmother called me at work and said, "You know he had cancer in his twenties?"

In the five years that I had been with him, no one felt that maybe, just maybe, I should have been told he was a cancer survivor? The simple prayer I stated at that moment was, "God Help Us!"

Later that day, a co-worker named Rosie stopped at my window to say she had something for me. She said, "When I saw these, I was compelled to purchase them for you."

I will never forget Rosie for her act of kindness. She handed me three silver charms made into unicorns. Unicorns have been a very special symbol to me. They reminded me that God and his Angels were watching over me. My eyes filled with tears, and Rosie looked embarrassed for a few moments. I shared with her what my husband's stepmother had told me and also what the unicorn meant to me. She left my office with a hug and a huge smile on her face.

I left work that afternoon and was to meet with my new business partner at my home. My partner in my new massage practice walked into my condo, stopped in her tracks, and took a deep breath. She looked stunned and beamed.

She said, "Tamara, I am sensing three Angels in our presence. They are letting me know that you need guidance and strength."

I told her they were probably there for my husband. Then I shared what I had been told about his health.

She stated, "They are here for you. He does not have cancer. Just wait and see."

I wanted to believe. I have always felt connected. I had lost my way. God reminded me not once, but twice that I was still connected. I was being reminded that God loved me, and I was being watched over and protected.

Before we were told that my husband did not have cancer, I ended up with pneumonia. Then he got pneumonia. Louise Hay's book, *You Can Heal Your Life*, would say I felt as if, "I did not have the right to breathe the air that I shared with others." The grief, the fear for my husband, and the new responsibility of my mother was overwhelming. Three months had not passed since my wedding. Things started to clear up. My business was picking up and my life started to look up. My husband did not have cancer. His disease was treatable. I was grateful.

I found out I was pregnant. We told no one. I had several pregnancies previously, and for whatever reason, I had no children. At the age of 35, I was both terrified and ecstatic. We went to a friend's wedding. During the wedding, the miscarriage started. My husband was devastated; he showed me a list of names he had written down.

He cried. I was stoic and stuffed my grief, as I had so many times before.

Two weeks later, the company he worked for acquired another business. The new business was in another state across the country. He was asked if he wanted to be a trainer. He left for over two months. After the first two weeks, he did not call. He occasionally answered my calls. When he came back, it took eighteen more months for the marriage to be completely over. Many horrible things were said and done in those eighteen months that left me without any self-confidence and zero self-worth.

Mystical experiences kept happening since the week my father passed away. I have had mystical experiences all my life, and it seemed there were more during this time. Angels have been part of my life since I was a little girl. I was three when the first Angelic awareness happened; they became my "imaginary friends." I was twenty-five when I died and physically met Angels for the second time. God kept reminding me that I was important. I started attending a local church, usually by myself. One day I entered the bookstore after church for no particular reason and no intention of purchasing anything. A book that was completely secured on its shelf and firmly between other books moved on it's own. It fell off the bookshelf and on to the top of my ankle.

A man who was standing next to me said with a big smile, "I think that one is yours!" The book was *The Messengers* by G. W. Hardin. The man said to me, "The book is about Nick Brunick and his experiences with angels and Jesus. Nick is going to be here at this church one night and at a local bookstore the next. He is visiting in two weeks. Possibly, you need to meet him. I definitely think you need to read the book."

I smiled, thanked him, rubbed my ankle, and picked up the book.

Since my father's death, I would sometimes hold a conversation with God and the room would just fill with brilliant colors. I started writing letters to my Angels and would get answers. I talked to God and later the Angels as if they were my personal, respected friends. I wrote a journal with all the fear, anger, anguish, and passion I had for my business and life. I wrote about the mystical experiences that were beyond my understanding. My understanding of the world was changing.

Several of my friends and I went to see Nick Brunick, the night he came into town. The room was filled with so much color. Tears just rolled down my face. The beauty in the room overwhelmed me. One of my friends, who benefited a great deal over the years from my mystical experiences, said to me, "You are not alone in this. We may not see what you see or feel, but we know it is truly happening."

The room had too many people who wanted to talk to Nick for me to speak with him that night. I knew that he was going to be at the local book store the next night. I was guided to make a copy of my journal and give it to him. There were so many very personal things in my journal, and I had no time to edit it. I needed someone who was having mystical experiences to understand what was happening to me. I was ashamed of some of the things I wrote and confused by others. I desperately needed help!

Several weeks passed until one day there was a letter from Nick. He stated that two things were clear: I was an Earth Angel and I needed to ask God for joy. As I sat there looking at the letter, I totally felt a connection to the Earth Angel statement. The comment on joy confused me. What is joy? I sat in disbelief, realizing I did not know what joy was! At that point in my life, I reflected back and came to an understanding I had never known what joy was.

I wrote this next prayer for myself and shared it with hundreds of people.

Prayer for Peace of Mind, Love, and Joy

Dearest Creator,

I give thanks for your presence in my life! I give thanks for my Guides and Angels. I give thanks that I am a servant of yours. I give thanks that I touch many people in a positive way. Creator, I don't understand why I battle with depression or why I am self-depreciating. I don't understand why I feel so lost sometimes or so empty and unworthy. God, I know the miracles You have sent me. I have seen them, and I have felt them. I ask that You open my eyes and heart to joy, love, and peace of mind. I ask that I be open to receive. As your servant, Creator, I understand and know that I am worthy.

So it is.

Tamara Michelle Dobbs

Simple Peace Prayer

Dearest_____,

I give thanks for your presence in my life. I give thanks that I am a servant of yours. I pray for peace of mind, love, joy, prosperity, and good health. With peace, I am no longer worried about my loved ones, my work, my home, my health, and my cash flow. With peace of mind and peace in my life, I know the love, joy, prosperity, and good health will follow. I ask that peace begins with me. Our world is in turmoil. If I am not at peace, how can I hope for peace in my community, in my nation, and in my world? Allow me to transcend all fears, depressed thoughts, and feelings of unworthiness.

Allow my life to be filled with love and joy and help me become a beacon of peace and love. I give thanks that I am a worthy servant.

I give thanks for the peace and love that is already coming to me in waves.

So it is!

There is no joy greater than a child's laugh.

CHILDREN AND THE LIFE CYCLE

HAVING CHILDREN

One of life's excruciating dilemmas is the desire by some to have children and the inability to conceive or carry a baby to term. This series of prayers is for people who want to be parents. I wrote this prayer for Lisa.

Dearest Creator,

I give thanks for You and my Guides and Angels. I give thanks for my friend Lisa and her Guides and Angels. Creator, Lisa is such an awesome Earth Angel. She brings joy to her work, and she brings joy as a friend and a wife. She radiates beauty inside and out. Her life, for the most part, is very full. There is one thing missing, God, and that is a child of her own. Lisa was one of many who were convinced to have a vaccination to protect her from a virus when she was younger. This "protection" is now proving to cause infertility issues. For Lisa and her husband, I pray that whatever is blocking Lisa from conceiving will be removed. I pray for an easy pregnancy for Lisa with a timely and easy birth resulting in a beautiful, healthy baby. God, we know that through You all things are possible.

So it is!

This little prayer that follows was difficult for me. I have always wanted a child; I have never been able to say, "Now is the time." My body has never cooperated when the timing might have worked. I laugh at myself as I am writing this. Each prayer that is done for another is also done for oneself. At my age and circumstance, now is definitely not the time.

This prayer is written as if you were praying for yourself. If the prayer is for someone else, just alternate the pronouns and add the person's name.

Simple Prayer for Conceiving a Child

Dearest_____,

I give thanks for my life, and I give thanks for You. I have one great sorrow. There is one thing missing and that is a child of my own. I pray that whatever is blocking me from conceiving be removed. I pray for an easy pregnancy with a timely and easy birthing that results in a beautiful, healthy baby. I know that through You all things are possible.

So it is!

Simple Prayer for Adopting or Fostering a Child

Dearest_____,

I give thanks for this day and for You. My prayer today is to increase my household by one, child. I ask, Creator, that there be a child who needs nurturing, correct discipline, and loving. My_____ and I believe we would be good parents. We ask that You send the right child to us. We ask that whatever legal or financial needs have to be met be simple and doable. We are ready for a family.

In your name, all is possible. So it is!

Simple Prayer on the Birth of a Child

Beloved_____,

Today is_____ 's first day of life. I ask that You wrap Archangel Michael's wings around this baby and keep him/her safe. I ask that You guide and direct the parents to raise her/him with love, compassion, wisdom, and integrity. I ask that this child know You and learn to be a good person. I ask that this child, with all of its possibilities, live life to the fullest with passion, joy, and laughter. I give thanks for this new life and being.

I pray that You bless their entire long life.

Sneaky Little Sucker this Thing Called Aging!

CAREGIVING AND AGING

Becoming disabled or attacked by a disease can happen at any age. If we are really lucky, someone who loves and adores us takes charge when we can no longer care for ourselves. Some of these duties may include, chauffeuring to doctor appointments, social workers, and attorney appointments. These duties may even be more time and energy invasive: cleaning, bathing, and feeding. When you become a caregiver for a loved one, your life goes on hold. My mother was my father's caregiver for almost ten years after he had his stroke. My sister-in-law and I became the caregivers for my mother.

Another group of caregivers needs to be mentioned here. It is not always possible for a family member to take care of a loved one. In my situation, as my mother's dementia set in and her mental stability became so off balance, in order to keep my own sanity and continue to work full time, I had to find a place close by for my mother to live in. This was a very hard decision to make. I found a place three miles from my home and work. I could and did drop everything when I was needed. Plus I saw her several times a week for many hours at a time. Sometimes there are no loved ones, and someone needs to show humanity by accepting a job to help those who no longer can help themselves. The caregivers on this planet have a special place in God's plan. I give personal thanks to those who assisted in the care and loving of my mother.

CAREGIVING

Dearest Creator,

I give thanks for your presence in the lives of my parents. I have watched my mother give over her life to care for my now disabled father. I ask that You help her find balance in his demands. My father's disability has made him grouchy and irritable. I ask that You help my mother understand that my father is frustrated because he was once a vital and a valued part of society. The loss of the use of half of his body and much of his vision has caused him to feel sorry for himself. He is needy and demanding and really cannot help himself. I ask that You reawaken my father's heart and compassion and help him realize what he is doing to his devoted wife. I pray for something to come into my father's life that gives him hope and helps him find an interest that he may focus on other than, "What is she doing?" I ask for my mother's peace of mind, balance, compassion, and love. Keep her safe and help her take care of herself so she may continue to do this heavy job that You have handed her. Surround her with your love.

Thank You, Creator!

Simple Prayer for Caregiving

Dearest _____,

I give thanks for your presence in our lives. _____ has become a caregiver of _____. _____ needs your help to deal with this new title of caregiver. Please help _____, balance time for her/himself, as taking care of _____ becomes the new focus of their lives. Give _____ the strength, courage, and compassion to deal with becoming a caregiver. I ask that Archangel

Michael be with them for protection and Archangel Raphael be with them for healing.

Thank You, and so it is.

AGING

Sneaky little sucker, this thing called aging. When I was younger, I did not understand when I saw an older person doing things that were not age appropriate. I did not know that the person inside still feels young. As you age, you don't lose the desire to climb mountains, ski, surf, dance, or have sex. Most of us simply lose the physical ability to participate in functions we once loved. I wrote this prayer for myself. If my words work for you, feel free to use them for yourself.

Dearest Creator,

    I give thanks for your presence in my awesome life. As your servant, Creator, I ask that You continue to guide and direct me during whatever time I have remaining in my life. I ask, Creator, that You help me be healthy and productive and to be of service to You. I ask that my aches and pains be minimal, so I may serve You at my best. I ask that when my time comes to join You that my passing is peaceful and without drama. I ask that those assisting me when I can no longer take care of myself are considerate and compassionate. I ask, Creator that You provide for me financially if the time comes that I need to be in assisted living or a nursing home. Lord, I ask that You help me age gracefully. As your servant, Creator, I give thanks that all will be taken care of.

    So it is.

Death is not death.
It is the address unknown and the unhuggables.
I feel your presence, and my beloved one, there
is no address where I may go to hug you!

DEATH AND HEALING

UNEXPECTED PASSING OF A CHILD

It has been a couple of tough years in losing family and friends. It began in February 2012 when my beautiful great niece lay down and died. She had stayed home from work because she thought she had the flu. Annie had a very large aneurysm. She was just a few weeks from being thirty. We miss you, Annie!

Recently, a young man that I heard about was with his friends when they all decided to jump off a bridge. His friends survived. He did not. He was sixteen years old.

I received a call from someone I know; one of her best friend's sons, had a seizure, hit his head, and was found three days later. He was not quite twenty.

A year ago, a girlfriend of mine called and stated her second cousin had drowned in the bathtub while her cousin walked away to answer the door. The cousin's child was two years old. A relative of mine had a healthy pregnancy. Ten minutes after this beautiful baby was born, the infant stopped breathing.

The last example I will use is an auto accident taking my friend's two great-grandchildren at the ages of thirteen and eighteen.

The one thing all of these situations had in common was unexpected death. Other things in common were that they ranged from ten minutes to thirty years old, very young in our eyes. Definitely too young to leave us.

We think, "What if? Could we have prevented it in some way? What were the last words we had with them? Were the words important? Did we tell them that we love them?"

This prayer was written as if the loss of the child was my own. In many ways, they were all my own. The simplified version is written for someone other than yourself.

Prayer upon the Death of a Child

Dear Lord,

How am I to stand the loss of my loved one, my child? I just saw them, spoke to them. What will I do now that I can no longer hug them or tell them that I love them? How can I stand breathing the air, knowing I no longer share the air with my beloved child? I keen, I wail, and I feel no relief. I miss my child's laughter, smile, and touch. My friends tell me I will feel less raw in time. I don't know how. I walk like a zombie, only doing what I must accomplish, then I become overzealous, neurotically doing everything at once. I feel so weak. Please, God give me peace, give me strength, and give me patience to deal with the misguided souls who say the wrong things unintentionally. Help me understand that I am not the only one grieving the loss of this child. I ask for compassion in my family and friends; it is hard to be kind when I hurt this bad. Creator, please forgive me for my anger at everyone, my anger at You. I cannot begin to say I understand your plan for us or your reasons for taking my child. Allow me to know that my beloved child is with You, safe and encased in your love. Please let my child know I love them. I will always love them. GOD HELP ME COPE!

Simple Prayer for Grief of Someone Else's Child

Dearest_____,

I give thanks for You; I give thanks for my friends and family. I ask for my friend/family member who has lost a child. I pray the child is with You, at peace and embraced by your loving presence. My friend/family member is in agony. It is hard enough to feel my own grief, much less feel the palatable pain _____ is emanating. I ask that through this soul-wrenching time, _____ 's family finds compassion for each other and not lash out in painful ways. I ask through You that my friend/family find solace and peace.

I give thanks that _____ is with You and not in pain. I give thanks for your presence in my friend's/family's lives. May they find peace and solace!

So it is!

PASSING OF A PARENT OF A YOUNG CHILD OR AN ADOLESCENT

The day I started out on the journey to write this book, one of my relative's ex-son-in-law was killed in a freak accident. He left behind two young boys, one aged nine and one aged eleven. When my beautiful great niece passed of an aneurysm, she left a beautiful little three year-old girl behind. And last year, one of my other great nephews, aged fifteen, lost his father to cancer. My family lost Tony, my brother-in-law, when I was five. He left behind four adult children from his first wife and three little girls from my sister. My three nieces and I were around the same age, and we grieved terribly.

It's very hard to explain to a child that their parent is not coming home. How do you explain that there will be no more hugs and kisses, and no more lap to sit on or stories to be told? Back in the sixties, children were not understood as well as they are today. The adults wailed and keened, and no thought was given to the fears and loss the child felt. Today, most adults think of children as little people with thoughts and feelings. I pray the parents consider grief counseling for these children. The counselor must be trained in pediatrics and have compassion and strength to help the children through this life-changing event.

Prayer for the Children who Lost Parents

Lord,

    I think of these children, and my heart weeps for them. I know they are thinking, "What will happen to me now? What will I do? How do I get my mother to stop crying?" I can almost hear these children think. God, I pray that You help these children come to terms with the loss of their father. Behavior issues that develop over the next years may be untreated grief. I pray that the remaining adults in their lives are astute enough to know these children need help. I ask, Creator that You help the adults clear up the legal issues and that these children will be provided for financially. I ask that You watch over these children. I pray they grow up in a loving, caring, and a financially secure environment.

I give thanks for your presence in their lives.

Simple Prayer for a Child Who Lost a Parent

Dearest _____,
My prayer today is for _____. This child/children has lost a parent. I feel their pain and confusion. I ask for your intervention.

I ask that You wake up an adult to see the level of fear they may be feeling.

I ask that You wrap yourself around _____, give this child/children peace,

and help them feel secure and loved. I ask that You surround this child/ children with Angels for protection and guidance. I give thanks for your presence in their lives.

So it is.

SUICIDE

Recently, a young woman was referred to me. Her mother was fearful that she was going to end her life. The young person had many very harsh lessons in life that were similar to some of my own. She had survived some horrendous experiences; they had made her strong and angry. Both of us had contemplated suicide because of the guilt and anger resulting from events in our youth.

I found strength in my belief in a higher power. I seek help every now and then when the world becomes too burdensome. My understanding of her pain and the years of training in meditation, prayer, and forgiveness work gave me some tools to help her. She felt hopeful at the end of the session.

One thing that has happened in both our lives is the suicide of people we knew. In my life, one was a nephew by marriage and the other was a friend. Karen has unfortunately had two family members pass away from suicide. Along with the healing session that I facilitated, I highly recommended she seek trauma counseling. The healing session began with the following prayer. The session included massage, Reiki (a healing energy modality), and hypnosis. This prayer was written for her later. May it now help someone else move through the guilt and pain! May it help someone find peace and hope!

PRAYER FOR A PERSON WHO HAS TAKEN THEIR OWN LIFE AND A PRAYER FOR THEIR FAMILY AND FRIENDS

Dearest Creator,

I give thanks for this opportunity for Karen and me to share. I give thanks for You, Creator, and our Guides and Angels. I give thanks for this healing session. Creator, I ask that anything that is heard during this session be heard from our hearts; our hearts feel anything that is felt and hear anything that is said. I ask, Creator that the energy in these hands comes from You and not me. I ask that Karen be protected from my stuff, and I am protected from her stuff. Creator, we ask that this session be for both of our greatest and highest goods.

Lord, Karen has had so much adversity and grief in her life; she has seen so much pain. I asked her to ask for joy in her life, and she broke into agonizing tears. She stated she did not know what joy was. Creator, You have entrusted two beautiful children into her care. They need their mother. These children need their mother to be whole, to hold on to her and feel grounded. They need to trust that she will be there for them as they grow older. We ask, Creator that You help Karen find peace, strength, and joy. We ask, Creator that You direct her to the right counselor who will ease her off the anxiety medications and help her find solace that those she loved are no longer in agony.

I ask that You have Archangel Michael wrap his wings around Karen and her two sons and mother. We ask that Archangel Raphael fill their hearts and bodies with the light of love to heal their torn souls. We ask that Archangel Gabriel help each of them speak, hear, and know the truth. I give thanks that Karen's family is being watched over by You and your minions. I give thanks that You are directing Karen to get the help that she needs. I give thanks that this session today gave her hope.

Blessings to all concerned.

Simple Prayer for Family and Friends Whose Loved One Took Their Own Life

Dearest _____,

I give thanks for You. I give thanks for knowing this loving family. My heart goes out to _____ in their time of grief. The pain of losing someone in this way is beyond belief. My prayer today asks that You help _____ find peace in their hearts and that answers as to why this happened are given to calm their souls. I pray they understand their loved one, _____, was in so much pain and now is with You and is pain free. I pray for those who would say taking one's own life destroys any chance of being with You in the heavens. I believe You are a loving _____ and no soul in agony would be turned away. This soul, _____, would be embraced with your love. Give them direction and help the family financially, since this untimely death may have caused a financial burden. Please bless this family with peace, strength, and understanding.

So it is!

Simple Prayer for a Person Who has Taken Their Own Life

Dear _____,

I just heard the news of a suicide. I know the family, and it breaks my heart to know their pain and to know that _____ was in so much pain, they could no longer bear it.

In my eyes, You are a loving God; because I believe this, I ask that You please help _____. I pray they are now with You and the Angels and You will provide _____ with what their soul needs.

Prayer When You Don't Have the Words

Please watch over _____ 's family and give _____ 's family strength, peace, and compassion for each other.

I send blessings to _____ 's family and bless _____' s soul.

MENTAL HEALTH

Many people today have mental health issues above and beyond depression and drug addictions. They may have schizophrenia, bipolar disorder, paranoia, or narcissistic or sociopathic tendencies. These people may have all or just some of these afflictions. Often the person suffering from mental "dis-eases" might not recognize that they are the one with the issue. The first prayer is for the friends and family who are suffering right along with the person who has the mental health issue. The second is for the person who is personally suffering with one or many mental health issues. Both are written in the simple form.

Simple Prayer for Friends and Family of Someone Who Has a Mental Disorder

Dearest _____,

I give thanks for your presence in my life and in the life of _____. I ask that You help me come to terms with _____ 's mental health issues. I pray for patience, compassion, and understanding. I need the inspiration to continue to hold my beloved one who is suffering in ways I cannot comprehend. I ask that You help me keep my sanity while I deal with _____ 's erratic behavior. Help me have appropriate and safe boundaries with this loved one. Protect me body, mind, spirit, and financially as _____ works though this darkness in their soul. Please help me have compassion without enabling. Give me strength and courage. Surround me with your love, so I may continue to love this troubled soul.

In your grace, all things are possible.

Simple Prayer for Someone Who has a Mental Disorder

Dearest _____,

    I give thanks that You are in _____ 's life. I ask that You help _____ through the darkness in their soul. They are lost and really do not understand (or because of their illness, even care) that their mental disorder is destroying other people's lives. I ask that You help us find appropriate help for _____ 's mental disease. I ask that whatever chemical imbalance they may have that something is found to assist in their healing. I am praying for a miracle. Please help _____ find their way back to a balanced way of thinking and living.

    In your name, all things are possible.

GRIEF AND DEVOTION

This prayer ties into the next prayer about sisters. I wrote it for my mother directly from my heart and my personal experience.

Dearest Creator,

I give thanks to Frances, my mother, for being in my life. I give thanks for the love we shared. My mother's final journey was a difficult road to walk for her and her family. The time we waited as she slipped into dementia and waited for her body to catch up with her mind was excruciating to watch. During that time, I doubted myself. I doubted if I was doing everything possible. I felt weak and overburdened with my day-to-day tasks of making a living and taking care of a person who often did not know my name in the last year of her life. I pray the time I invested was not in vain. I ask forgiveness for the times I just wished it were over. Now that the suffering is over, I pray that my mother, Frances, be at peace and that I find peace in knowing that she has gone home to You.

Lord, I ask that You help me let go of the guilt of not doing enough, caring enough, or loving enough. I gave everything I possibly could, and then I reached inside and found through You I had more to give. I ask that I no longer feel guilty for feeling relief. The suffering went on so long. Creator, I understand that my mother is at peace and in your protection. I now ask for peace for myself, so I may go on with the remainder of my life.

I give thanks knowing that it is so!

Simple Prayer for Releasing Grief of a Loved One that You Have Attended and Devoted Yourself To

Dear _____,

This last journey of _____ has been a difficult road for my family. The time that I waited and served, never knowing how long it would be or if I was doing everything possible, I pray it was not in vain. I ask for forgiveness for the times I just wished it were over. Now that the suffering is over, I pray that _____ be at peace and that I find peace in knowing _____ has gone home to You. I ask that You help me let go of the guilt of not doing enough, caring enough, or loving enough. I gave everything I possibly could, and then I reached inside and through You I found more to give. I ask that I not feel guilty for the relief. The suffering went on for so long. I give thanks that the suffering has ended. Through You, I accept what my role has been in _____'s journey.

Thank You! So it is.

SISTERS

Two sisters provided service for their mother and each other. The burden was heavy; the grief left one with a broken heart and shoulders bent with the burden. I met May in a grocery store. May had a migraine that was just ruining her day. I told her I could get rid of it for her. She had a wrist brace on, and I questioned her about it. Within minutes, she told me her story. She started with the surgery she was having in days on the TFCC ligament, and her sister would be having surgery days later to alleviate pressure on the brainstem from a stroke. May was frightened for both of them.

May's sister Carol had full responsibility for taking care of their mother, while May worked to keep food on the table and a roof over their heads. Carol ate healthy foods, exercised, and ran to stay at optimum health. Shortly after their mother died, Carol had an extensive heart attack, brokenhearted from grief. Sometime later, Carol had a stroke. The stroke left her body bent. This proud, athletic woman now holds her head and shoulders as if the burden she carries is more than she can stand. Here is my prayer for these loving sisters.

DEVOTION AND HEALING

Dear God,

I give thanks for your presence in my life and your presence in the lives of May and her sister Carol. I give thanks for their Guides and Angels. Their journeys have been difficult. The passing of their mother several years ago left a huge void in their lives. May and Carol need help releasing all guilt and feelings of inadequacy associated with their mother's care and journey to You.

May has been injured and needs surgery. Creator, we ask that the doctors, anesthesiologist, and surgery team are knowledgeable, efficient, aware, and first-rate. Lord, please help the operating team be the best!

We ask, Creator that May have the time and help she needs during her full complete and easy recovery. We accept this healing!

Lord, we also ask that You watch over May's sister, Carol. Carol's service to You and her family as the caregiver for her mother was the best she could provide. Carol honored the temple that You gave her (her body). She gave it good food and exercise and lived in a healthy manner. Unfortunately, the care of and loss of her mother put a great strain on Carol's heart and circulatory system, creating a heart attack and more recently a stroke. Carol now holds her head on her shoulders as if there is a great burden. Creator, we ask that the burden be lifted. Through Christ, Carol understands she did all that she could.

Carol was and is an excellent daughter and sister. We ask, Creator that Carol has a healing of her body, mind, spirit, and soul. We ask that the answers the new physicians have discovered are fixable.

May and Carol are still young. Creator, we ask that their remaining years on this planet be filled with peace of mind, love, joy, prosperity, and better health.

In Christ's name, so it is!

Simple Prayer Asking for Healing the Body and Injury of Someone Other than Yourself

Dearest _____,

I give thanks for your presence in my life. I give thanks for your presence in _____ 's life. I give thanks for _____ 's Guides and Angels. _____ has had an injury and is in need of surgery. I ask that the surgeon, anesthesiologist, and the surgery team is knowledgeable, efficient, aware, and first-rate.

I ask that _____ have the time and help they need during their full, complete, and easy recovery.

We ask that _____ accepts this healing.

In your name all is possible!

LOST LIMBS AND PARALYSIS

Losing a limb or the use of a limb can cause deep depression and possibly suicidal thoughts. My grandfather on my father's side lost an arm before he was thirty. My father became a paraplegic at age fifty-six. My father went into a deep depression when he came out of his coma from his stroke. The week before I decided to write this book, a young woman who had lost part of her foot was brought in for a Reiki healing session. The young woman appeared to her family as adjusting very well to her loss. I recommended to her family that the young woman attend grief counseling.

Simple Prayer for Loss of Use of Limb or Paralysis

Dearest _____,

_____ has lost the use of _____. The loss has been tremendous. First the emotional and then the financial loss of no longer having the use of _____ has been devastating.

I ask that You help _____ body, mind, spirit, soul, and financially come to terms with this great loss. Help _____ find peace and be able to move forward. Help those of their support team understand that pity is not needed. Help _____'s family be kind to each other during this time of loss. Wrap Archangel Raphael's wings around _____ to facilitate healing. I give thanks that your Angels are already working on this issue.

So it is.

SOMEONE WITH A LIFE THREATENING ILLNESS

I wrote this prayer for a young woman named Ashley. 20 months before the prayer was written, Ashley's older brother passed away. He was four years older than she was. His cancer was genetic.

Prayer for Ashley

Dearest Creator,

I don't always understand why things happen. What is happening to Ashley and her family is one of the toughest life experiences a human can go through. I ask for Ashley's family to find peace. I pray for a healing that goes beyond the body. I ask that You surround her and her family in love. I ask that You send them financial prosperity to ease the burden of the medical procedures. I ask that the remaining siblings be healthy. I pray that the physicians are wrong and that there is a cure. If not a cure, a miracle. I ask that even in adversity that Ashley and her family find joy.

Through Christ, all things are possible!

Ashley was one of seven children. Three had been diagnosed and suffered. Four are in the clear. Besides Ashley and her brother, a third child was diagnosed with the genetic marker. When this child hit puberty, this rare form of cancer assaulted her little body. She knew what was coming; the whole family and many of her friends knew it. This family is a deeply religious, spiritual family. What this family has been through has strengthened their beliefs.

Prayer for a Miraculous Cure

Dearest Creator,

I give thanks for this blessed day; I give thanks for You and this opportunity to pray for Melissa. Melissa is just a small child, seven years old. Lord, she has been through so much in her few years on this planet. She has watched two of her siblings be diagnosed with a rare genetic form of cancer. She has watched them fight the cancer and then watched them die. Six months before the death of her sister, Melissa was tested and told she had the genetic marker. Unless there is a cure or miracle, she is doomed with the same fate.

God, please give our scientists the knowledge to discover a cure for this rare form of cancer. I pray that You give the family the strength to stay together, to find strength in each other, to be kind to each other. I ask that no one in the family feel guilty for being here when the others are not. Please wrap Archangel Michael's wings around Melissa and her family for protection. Bring Archangel Raphael in to their family for healing and Archangel Gabriel for finding, hearing, speaking, and knowing the truth. Please, bless Melissa and her family!

So it is!

Before this book was sent to publishing, Ashley and Melissa passed. Same cancer.

SIMPLE PRAYER FOR A CURE OF A LIFE THREATENING DISEASE

Dearest _____,

I give thanks for your light and your love in my life. I am praying for _____ who has a life threatening disease. I am asking for a miracle. I am asking that a cure be found for (disease) and made readily available to all those who need it. I ask that our scientists and those who support them find it within their hearts to share and make affordable this cure to all who need it. In truth, I am asking for two miracles.

In your name, ALL is possible. So it is.

MERCY WITH DEATH

by Frances Dobbs (1921-2014)

Make me tired enough that I won't mind,
To leave the moon and all the stars behind.
That it won't sadden me to know,
I'll not again see winter's first soft fall of snow.
Make me so weary of it all,
That I won't miss the robin's call,
Or feel endless aching loneliness,
To be without the wind's caress,
When I leave this beauty,
Though I'll not forget;
Let me lose my want to hold it...
Leave me no regret.

God bless our public servants.
They give so much and many give the ultimate sacrifice.

SERVICEMEN, WOMEN, AND TYRANNY PROTECTORS OF OUR COUNTRY AND MILITARY

PROTECTORS OF OUR COUNTRY AND MILITARY

Every time I see a young man or woman in a military uniform, I thank them for their service. In the moment, if there is time, I attempt to engage in a comfortable conversation. I ask about their family. I ask if they are on leave or going back to where they are deployed. I ask if they are dining by themselves. When they ask for their bill, they find it has been paid. Because of the turmoil and horror some of these young men and women see and experience, they need to know we appreciate them and see them as human beings. Many men in my family have donated their time and lives to the armed forces. Currently, we have no family members in the armed forces.

Prayer for Those who Protect our Country

Dearest Creator,

I am so thankful to live in this glorious country where I can speak my mind and listen to others speak their minds. I give thanks for those who fought against tyranny and won. It's hard for me to say I give thanks that men and women gave their lives for my freedom. It saddens me that any lives are given to fight for freedom that should already be ours. It is human to want more: more power, more money, and more land. It is human for mankind to believe that You are the only one that is right. It seems to be a human trait to fight to be right. This is where human strife comes in. This is where we need our highly trained service men and women. We need them to be your servants, Creator. We need them to defend our freedom, to be the peacekeepers for other countries. I give the deepest thanks to those young men and women who have and will give their lives for our freedom. I give deep thanks for those men and women who have seen too much. Their souls are burdened with what they have seen and have been asked to do. I ask, Creator that You watch over our men and women during their tours of duty. I pray that when these men and women come home, they are able to receive help with their medical and psychological needs. I ask that You help our service men and women find solace in You. I pray they find peace in knowing what they were ordered to do, what they needed to do was for our country's greatest and highest good. I give thanks for their sacrifices.

May they be blessed!

Simple Prayer for our Service Men and Women

Dearest _____,

I am so thankful to live in this glorious country where I can speak my mind and listen to others speak their minds. I give thanks for those who fought against tyranny and won. We need our service men and women to be your servants. We need them to defend our freedom and be the peacekeepers for other countries. I give the deepest thanks to those young men and women who have and will give their lives for our freedom. I give deep thanks for those men and women who have seen too much. Their souls are burdened with what they have seen and have been asked to do. I ask that You watch over our service people. I ask that You help our service men and women find solace in You. I pray they find peace in knowing what they were ordered and needed to do was for our country's greatest and highest good. I give thanks for their sacrifices.

May they be blessed!

PRISONERS OF WAR AND THOSE MISSING IN ACTION

I was recently invited to "The Spirit of 45" event. This is a celebration of the World War II veterans and the ending of World War II on August 14, 1945. The celebration and memorial happens every year on the second Sunday of August. Men and women well into their late eighties, nineties, and even in their hundreds were honored. One of the most touching speeches and commemorative moments was the honoring of the POWs and MIAs. Tears flowed freely from many in the audience. This prayer is for those who are prisoners of war and for those who we may never know where they are or what has become of them.

Prayer for Prisoners of War and Those Missing In Action

Lord,

I don't understand war. I do not understand man's ability to be cruel and inhumane to each other. I don't understand the needless murder and torture that people are capable of. For what reason? Money, land, jealousy, and religious beliefs? Countless mothers, fathers, brothers, sisters, husbands, wives, and lovers have huge voids in their lives. Many service men and women have been lost behind enemy lines. They have experienced immeasurable atrocities.

God,

I ask that You help the families find answers as to where their young men and women are and what has happened to them. I pray, Creator that You open the hearts of their captors, our enemies, and allow our people to come home. If it is not possible, I ask, Creator that information as to the whereabouts of our lost service men and women are shared with their families and friends. Christ, for those who are still living, I ask that you wrap your love and protection around them, filling them with courage and strength until they are released. Bring them home, please.

I give thanks that through You everything is possible.

Simple Prayer for our Service MIA and POW Service Men and Women

Dear _____,

I have a loved one who served our country. My loved one has not been heard from in quite some time. The military has stated they are MIA/POW. This not knowing, this hoping that they will walk through the door with open arms and tears to embrace me, is more than I can stand. Please, allow me to know what has become of my loved one. If you cannot send them back to me, please help me find peace with the answers.

Thank You.

Prayer for Men and Women Who Have Been Falsely Imprisoned

Creator,

I give thanks for my awesome country. I give thanks for the freedom that comes with living in my country. I have a prayer for people who are unjustly being held prisoner. These people made mistakes that cost them months or years in prison by being in the wrong place at the wrong time. Their situations were mishandled from the start.

Creator, I beseech You to open all the hearts of those who believe they are in control of these humans' plights. I ask that these people be released to their families alive and healthy. I ask for common sense to prevail. I ask for a miracle.

I turn this over to, You, Lord. So it is!

POLICE MEN AND WOMEN

When I was somewhere between the ages of five and seven, we had a police officer who was assigned to protect our neighborhood. His name was John. He was a big man, as big as John Wayne was. My family lived in a small town where everyone knew each other. Our John, as my father called him, did not always arrest the miscreant teenagers when he found them doing something not quite legal. John would often get them in his car and take them to their home to let justice be settled there. He was at our home several times because of one of my siblings. My father stated it was like watching a mother cat pick up her kitten by the scruff of the neck and put them in a safer place. I felt safe knowing he was out there watching after my siblings and me. It was a time when common sense and compassion prevailed. It was a sad night when we heard that John's gun went off while he was getting out of his car. The bullet went through the artery in his leg, and he died before he could get out of his car. We were told the safety on his gun was defective.

The job of a police person is a sacred position. These people who lay their lives on the line almost to be superhuman. They have to assess every situation. Is this a robbery? Is it an armed robbery? Is it a drug deal? Is it a lover's quarrel? Is the situation a life-threatening situation? What kinds of reinforcements, if any, do I need? Police officers have to know the base side of human nature and still be able to access common sense. They have to be tough but still have the ability to have compassion. Many people are taught to fear the police, and the police have been taught not to trust most people. With fear and distrust, there is always potential for someone to get hurt.

Reminder: For the simplified prayer, please change the word Creator to whatever name of God works for you.

Prayer for Police

Dearest Creator,

    I give thanks for your presence in my life. I give thanks that law and order is a foundation for my life. I am praying for a group of people who have to uphold law and order, our police forces. These men and women, who put their lives on the line to help keep order in our communities, need your protection, Creator. I ask that their Patron Saint Michael keep them safe, especially from those who would kill or maim for no apparent reason. I ask that You keep them safe during traffic stops. I ask, Creator, that You fill them with the ability to see through the worst con artist and still have compassion for a first time offender who just got caught up in a prank. I give thanks for the police men and women who put their lives on the line every day for the safety of our community. I give thanks that You watch out for them and protect them.

    Thank You. So it is!

FIREMEN AND WOMEN

Months before 9/11 happened, I started having dreams that were frightening. I am extremely intuitive and just could not figure out why I was having horrible dreams. The dreams were tempered by an angelic presence, otherwise they would have been too horrific to tolerate. Because of the dreams, I started making dream catchers. Each dream catcher became a piece of art. I sold a few and became obsessed with making more and more. My massage practice at one time I had thirty dream catchers hanging from the ceiling. 9/11 happened. Within the next six months, I made more dream catchers. I was no longer selling them. I was giving them away. It amazed me how many of my clients, friends, and family were somehow involved in a business in the towers or at the Pentagon. One of my clients had firefighters in her family that had been involved rescuing people in the trade towers. My client loved the dream catchers and asked me to make one for her grandchildren who were having night terrors. I made one for each child and for the parent's room. It did not seem right to charge for these dream catchers. The average dream catcher took four to eight hours each to make and depending on the size and content, $15 to $100 in supplies. I then started giving away the dream catchers to anyone who had family involved in the disaster in New York. Many of my dream catchers reached families of fire men and women in New York. I give thanks for the dedication of all the first responding firemen and women, police, EMS, and everyone who contributed to helping in our nation's great time of need.

Prayer for Firefighters

Dearest Creator,

I give thanks for the men and women who are highly trained and willing to run into burning buildings in order to save our homes, pets, and lives. I ask that You protect these men and women. I pray that their equipment works perfectly and that they are able to sense when it is time to move out of harm's way and when it is alright to go forward to save lives. I ask that You have Archangel Michael wrap his protective wings around each and every fire person when they enter a dangerous situation, whether toxic chemicals or fire. I give thanks for their presence and for your presence in their lives.

FIRST RESPONDERS AND EMS

On December 11, 1985 at 2:30 in the afternoon, my mother and I left our home to go Christmas shopping, eat dinner, and play bingo. We made it to the end of the block and just around the corner, a Mack truck filled with industrial parts hit us head on. The whole event is a book unto itself. It changed my life and how I see the world and the other side. It also created my belief in Angels. God put a first responder at the accident who actually knew me. At first, I had no vital signs. My mother was trapped in the car. I was told that I was put aside and covered with a blanket, written off. The concern at the time was to save the lady still alive and trapped in the car.

That is what I was told happened. If anyone knows any differently, I am open to hearing their version. When it was discovered who was laying on the ground under the blanket, the young man who knew me refused to let me go. Because God put him there and because the Angels on the other side gave me a choice to stay with them or come back to Earth, I am here today. Thank you, EMS.

Simple Prayer for First Responders

Dearest _____,

I give thanks for the men and women who come upon a scene of a tragedy and actively throw common sense out the door to do whatever it takes to save lives. I ask that You watch over these special people. Please continue to give them the courage and strength to face other people's misfortunes. I ask that You help these men and women sleep at night without having to see or relive the events in their dreams. I ask that they have peace of mind. If the people or animals they save cannot or forget to say thank you, I pray that somehow You let them know how much we appreciate the hard work and sacrifices they make in order to help those of us who are experiencing tragedy.

Thank You for the lives that you allow them to save!

LEADERS: LOCAL, STATE, NATIONAL, AND WORLD

I am not very political, so my friends who are fanatical in their partisanship, often drives me crazy. Both sides believe I should take a side. I learned not to ask why. Their passion and negativity attached to their belief is often toxic. My way is not liberal, right, or left. It is compassionate with appropriate boundaries and common sense.

Simple Prayer for our Local and State Leaders

Dearest _____,

I give thanks to You. I am praying for the leaders of our local governments. Help us find the right people for the positions to enhance and stabilize our community and state. Please help us make intelligent decisions about whom we vote for, to be our local governing force. I ask that we be given the strength and ability to not be complacent when our political servants do our people wrong. I am asking that You watch over our leaders; help them govern with honesty, justice, commonsense, strength, and compassion. I ask that we can see through all deceit and dishonesty in the leaders who are not governed or guided by You. I ask that our government leaders put the people first rather than letting their personal agendas supersede what is the best for the populace and their constituents.

I give thanks as I turn these people and these positions over to You!

Prayer for our National Leaders

Dearest _____,

I give thanks for You in my life. I give thanks that this country was based on religious freedom and separation of church and state. I give thanks because we are founded on religious freedom. I pray that You are in the hearts of those who lead our country. I pray that whatever deceit is happening in our nation's capital shows itself. I ask that we the people find a way to make our voices heard. I ask that our government leaders put the people first rather than letting their personal agendas supersede what is the best for the populace. We have had enough. Without pointing fingers. I don't think any man or woman knows what is really going on in our nation's capital, I call upon your legion of Angels to show our leaders the right things they need to do. I call upon these Angels to open our leaders' hearts to living in integrity. I call upon our Angels to protect the leaders who are making the right choices. I ask that You help the "common man" see through the misinformation. I ask that when we finally see the truth as it is and not how it is shown that we have the ability, strength, and courage to correctly take action to rectify our problems. It is time that our country's leaders are led and inspired by You. In _____ name, all things are possible!

TERRORISM

Every night, every day, it seems we are seeing and hearing about another act of terrorism. Young women being abducted, raped, tortured, and killed. A journalist simply doing his or her job and being beheaded is unacceptable. Hatred in the name of God does not justify the killings. We must pray for the end of the hideous acts. It's time for "we the people of all nations" to say enough! We will no longer accept or tolerate terrorism.

Ending Terrorism

Dearest Creator,

I give thanks for You and our Angels. I give thanks for this beautiful world You have given us to live in. I give thanks for the kindness and love that I have grown up with. Creator, we humans have a problem. Books that were written centuries ago are being interpreted by radical groups of men and women who state that if others do not follow their book to the letter of their law, we all must die. I see You as a loving God, not a vengeful God. Lord, I want the senseless killing to stop. I ask Creator that You touch the hearts of those who can stop the insanity. I ask Creator, for protection from our enemies. I ask for peace for a group of people who believe that they are the only ones to know You. They believe that by knowing You and your mind that they have not only the right but the need to destroy all that gets in their way. Please help our world. Help mankind find kindness in our hearts.

I know that through Your name, all things are possible.

WAR AND PEACE

At any given point in time there are approximately 30 ongoing conflicts in the world, ranging from drug wars, terrorist insurgencies, ethnic conflicts and civil wars. At the time of this writing there are two that have taken the center stage of horror. Russia/Ukraine and Israel and Plestine. Our news is flooded with the atrocities of people against people. A few reasons are greed, religious beliefs, political beliefs and land. Dear Lord, Children and other innocents around the world are being attacked and murdered. Torture, kidnapped, raped, bombings are happening and targetting the weakest. The atrocities have been happening since the beginning of time. All involved are suffering and for what? God we need you and your love to fill those who would hate and feel that their needs and wants are more important than other peoples lives with common sense and compassion.

Prayer for the Israel and Palestine Conflict:

Author Bill Hernandez

God of Love and Mercy,

We come to you in prayer for the people of Israel and Palestine. We ask for your guidance and wisdom to help bring an end to the violence and conflict that has plagued this region for so long. We pray for the safety and protection of all those caught in the crossfire, and for the families of those who have lost loved ones. We pray for the leaders of both sides, that they may be moved by your spirit to seek peace and reconciliation. We ask that you soften their hearts and help them to see the humanity in each other, so that they may work together towards a just and lasting peace. We pray for the international community, that they may use their influence to support efforts towards peace and justice. We ask that you give them the courage to speak out against violence and oppression, and to work towards a future where all people can live in peace and security. God of Hope, we pray for the cities and towns of this region, that they may be places of safety and refuge for all who live there. We ask that you bless the people of Israel and Palestine with the strength and resilience to rebuild their lives and communities in the aftermath of conflict. We pray for your peace to reign in this land; and for your love to overcome all hatred and division. We ask all of this in the name of Jesus Christ, the Prince of Peace. Amen.

SOUTH AMERICA AND THE CHILDREN'S CRISIS

Witten in 2012

There is something going on that our government and our newscasters and reporters are either missing or choosing to ignore. Why are people exiting South America by the thousands? Some reports say the exodus is one thousand or more a day. Some reports state that children are entering our country without adults, hundreds at a time, children caring for children. Why? Some would say the grass is greener. This would make sense if it were just adults and their children. Why, in some cases, are there children without adults? Where are their parents? What or who is chasing them out? What is making them so afraid that they would risk death to escape? This topic causes a lot of anger amongst my friends. This prayer is for those persecuted, homeless, and afraid. Many of my friends will be angry with my choice of words and phrases in this next prayer. My goal is not to make enemies; my goal is to come from my heart. (I wrote this prayer in 2014 for the first time.)

Prayer for South American Refugees Written in 2012

Lord,
    Today I give thanks that I live in a country that for the most part is free from persecution. I give thanks that there are jobs, decent places to live, good water and good food. I give thanks that you have watched over our country and guided many of our leaders.
    Something is out of balance, Creator, and I am not in the right place to know or understand why or what the reason for the imbalance

is. Our neighboring country, Mexico, has many excellent resources. If they chose to use those resources appropriately, they would have as many possibilities to grow and prosper as our country has. For some reason, Mexico's population is fleeing across the border to our country, apparently putting a stress on our economy. We are not a poor nation, and we are not heartless. Our people have been struggling in a way that they are not used to. Our people have become fearful that there are not enough resources for our own people. Because of this, many Americans believe the hordes of people coming over the border are disease ridden freeloaders instead of refugees who are under attack.

Creator, I ask that the truth come out. I ask that if tyranny is the problem and the problem can be solved by removing the tyrant, I ask that Mexico's people and the free world's governments take action to end the tyranny.

I ask that the children with and without parents are protected. I ask, Creator, that those who have disease be treated and cared for in a loving, compassionate way. I pray the children who no longer have parents are matched with people who would truly love and care for them. Creator, it breaks my heart that these children for whatever reason are separated from their parents. I admire the will to live and courage you have instilled in them. In Jesus' name, I ask this crisis be solved. Blessed are the children.

TYRANNY

I heard of a healer who once lived in Uganda. Uganda was in a civil war during his childhood. Mercenaries murdered one of his brothers in front of him. He was only 12 at the time. The future healer was initiated as an adult and forced to become a mercenary. Somewhere along the line, he was accepted into the United States under political asylum. Today he is a very gifted healer.

Simple Prayer for People in a War Torn Country

Dear _____,

My prayer today is for people who live in countries where there is tyranny and destruction. I cannot imagine living in an environment where I am afraid to speak my mind or walk down the street. I cannot imagine living where men in uniform inhabit the streets with machine guns. I cannot imagine living in a place where the children have little food and it is not safe for them to play outside. This is a place where children do not play with toy guns, but learn to use real guns and are put out to fight a war. Please end the atrocities to men, women and children, created by men of greed and a greater need for power.

Dearest _____,

I ask that You help humankind to wake up. I ask that children have the opportunity to play and grow in a safe environment. I ask that women find within themselves the courage to come together and say ENOUGH! And I ask that the women help their mates understand that peace is necessary to survival. I am asking for a miracle. I am asking for it now!

Through You all things are possible!

*It's five o'clock somewhere Mommy's little helper.
Not all addicts are who you think they are.*

ADDICTIONS, NEIGHBORS, AND GOD

GETTING DRUG DEALERS OUT OF YOUR NEIGHBORHOOD

In this day and age, drug addiction is one of the toughest things we humans have to deal with. Neighborhoods that were once safe, have a virus that slithers in between the cracks and takes root before we are aware of what is happening. It grows slowly at first then vengefully destroys our peace. Like cancer, drug addiction grows. I have written these prayers as if they were for me personally.

Prayers for the Drug Addicts and Dealers

Dearest Creator,

    I would like to say thank You for being in my life. I give thanks for You and my Guides and Angels. What a mess we have here. We need some help in our neighborhood. Not too long ago, the neighbors in our area were good quality people. They made good healthy decisions for their families, working hard to earn an honest living. Within the last three years, this has changed. A young woman moved into our neighborhood. She was injured on a job, and everyone's life around her changed. She became addicted to oxycodone. Her life began to revolve around getting this drug for her pain. Then she started to sell drugs. The neighborhood changed as more drug dealers and buyers moved into the area. I do not want to be angry; I do not want to feel resentful. I do not want to fight. I do not want to be in fear of losing my life or the life of anyone in the neighborhood. I ask, Creator that this young woman learn her lesson and move on. I pray that she finds her way out of the drug induced mess she is in. I pray those who Are negatively influencing this young woman, move out of her life I send blessings to all.

    So it is!

Tamara Michelle Dobbs

Prayer for Protection of the Neighborhood and Self

Creator,

I ask for protection. My association with someone who will not stand against the destruction of the neighborhood has put me in harm's way. I agree with the person and the other people who are standing up for our neighborhood. When the time is right, I am right by their side saying, "Enough!"

Until recently, I was the mediator and voice of reason and compassion. I do not agree with how others are handling the situation. People keep stirring up a hornet's nest, making it worse. I was assaulted and spit on in my own yard. My car was also damaged. I was not physically hurt. The police officer who was called seemed uninterested in taking any action beyond a strong lecture to the perpetrator. I felt violated and helpless.

I am afraid, Creator. I am afraid for my friends in the neighborhood. I am afraid for my home, car, animals, my mate's and my life. I am uncomfortable with fear. Because of my strong faith in You, fear is not an emotion I feel very often. I am not a vengeful person. I ask for protection from these people.

I ask that You have Archangel Michael wrap his protective wings around me and around the neighbors who are standing up for what is right. Keep us all safe. I ask that Archangel Raphael is present in all of our lives to help heal what is out of balance. Archangel Gabriel, make the truth known to all. In Christ's name, all things are possible.

Simple Prayer for Drug Addicted Neighbors

Dearest _____,

I am normally a peaceful person. I give thanks for You, my friends, and my family. Recently, some turmoil has entered into my life. This turmoil has been brought into my neighborhood through misuse, abuse, and sales of legal and illegal drugs. I pray that You protect the children in this neighborhood. Protect the property values, households, and the neighborhood watch. I pray for the addicts. I pray they find help for their bodies, minds, spirits, and souls. If they are unable or unwilling to get help healing from their addiction, I ask that they be removed from our neighborhood and moved elsewhere.

I give thanks that You already have your Angels working on this for the greater good of all concerned.

So it is!

CORRECT DECISION MAKING

Jason is a brilliant young man. He graduated with honors from high school and had several opportunities to pick and choose from many elite universities. He decided to take a year off to work and play. The year cost him all of the potential scholarships. It also cost him a year on probation for a small amount of marijuana. He managed to go to college on his own where he met a girl who was mentally unstable. She had accused three of her last boyfriends of rape; two of them were doing time. Jason knew about the two, one in prison and one in jail. A major red flag that he ignored. He was the fourth she had arrested for rape. He was exonerated. It was proven he was in another city the day the rape was supposed to have happened. He was arrested for unrelated charges during the stressful time of the investigation. In less than two years, Jason was arrested for marijuana, rape, and a DUI. Somewhere along the line, life started going well for him. He got a very good job. The company stood by him through his entire ordeal. One day he quit his job. He has quit every job he has had since and is putting a great burden on his family.

Jason's poor choices were driving his family insane. His family asked me to pray for him.

Prayer for Correct Decision Making: Let Go and Let God

Dear God,

I am writing this prayer for Jason. I have known him since he was nine. He is now twenty-six. I have listened to the praise from his family for this brilliant young man. As he has grown, I have been just as proud of him as if he were my own son.

Jason is now struggling with the poor decisions he has made. It seems he is in a self-destruct mode. As this young man's surrogate aunt, I ask that he be shown a way out of his downward spiral before it is too late. I pray that You open his eyes and all his senses so he may understand and know when he is in the process of making a poor choice. I ask, Creator that You have his Guardian Angels speak loud enough and with enough force with a vision of what will happen if he continues with the bad choices he is making. I know this is possible. I ask that You make your presence known to Jason. I ask that You fill his soul with peace, love, understanding, and compassion for himself and his family. I ask that You wrap Archangel Michael's wings around Jason to protect him. I ask Archangel Raphael to heal whatever is out of balance in his life. I ask Archangel Gabriel to help Jason learn to speak, hear, and know the truth. I turn Jason over to You, Creator. I give thanks that all things are possible through You.

So it is!

Simple Prayer for Correct Choices

Dearest _____,

This prayer is for _____ and for the choices he/she is making. I ask that _____ see the current path is only spiraling down. I ask that _____ realize he/she needs help. I ask, Creator that You open the heart and eyes of _____. I ask that You surround _____ with your love. I ask that her/his Guides and Angels make your wishes for this person heard and felt loud and clear. I ask that You find a way to make your presence known in _____ 's life. I know that through You all is possible. I turn _____ over to You.

So it is!

Tamara Michelle Dobbs

Simple Prayer for Letting Go and Letting God

Ah _____,

    I am overwhelmed with worry for _____. I know he/she is on a path that is spiraling down. I love this person so much it hurts my heart to witness what is happening. I ask _____ that he/she learn their lessons. I know You are guiding this person. I feel as if they are not listening to anyone, including You. If I keep feeling this way and obsessing with _____ 's behavior, I know that I will be of no help to others or myself. I am asking for peace that surpasses understanding. I send love and compassion to _____, and I turn my expectations for their lives over to You. I give Thanks for the peace that you fill my heart with.

    I LET GO AND I LET _____! So it is!

To take a journey is to be on an adventure!

JOURNEYS AND NEW BEGINNINGS

MOVING ON

It might seem odd to start this next section with prayers to sell homes and find new jobs. I am certain that the people in these next prayers would not be experiencing new beginnings on their journeys without releasing old thought patterns.

This next prayer was written as one prayer for two different couples who needed similar results for different reasons. The simplified prayer is split into two different prayers.

The first couple's children have all moved out of state. He is retired and she is unable to obtain a job in the local area. They have found a home in another state, closer to their children and her family in the north. They currently live in a state that has hurricanes, but they cannot get enough insurance on their current residence if one should pass through. At the time of this writing, it is currently hurricane season. The home is under 1,300 square feet and immaculate. The home is updated and in perfect working order.

The second couple started out with two homes: one in Florida and the other in Missouri. Over a seven-year period, they inherited two other homes. They want to keep their home in Florida, sell her mother's home that they have been renting, sell their home in Missouri, and keep their inherited home in Wisconsin. This couple is in their late 60s, with some minor health issues. The stress of what to do with four homes is taking a toll. They loved their parents deeply. Dealing with all the complications that come with the death of loved ones along with the question of what to do with the loved ones' belongings has been quite tiring.

Both prayer requests came to me within an hour of each other.

Prayer for Selling Property and Moving Forward

Dearest Creator,

I give thanks for You, my Guides and Angels. I am writing this prayer for three separate households, two separate couples. The condo on Mountain Lion Court, the second house in Missouri belonging to Mia and Jason, and Bruno and Theresa's house on River Rock Road need to sell as soon as possible. I ask that it be for everyone's greatest and highest good that they sell quickly. Earth time quickly! I ask that the properties sell for the price asked and that the deals close within a month or less of contracts being signed. I ask that the closings also go smoothly. I ask, Creator that once everything is settled, the owners of the properties have enough time to remove their personal items from the premises without causing great stress on the couples.

I give thanks that this action, this prayer is for everyone's greatest and highest good.

So it is!

Simple Prayer for Selling Property out of Necessity

Dearest _____,

I give thanks for your presence in my life. As your servant, I am praying for my friends/family in the sale of their home. A time has come that the home they live in must be released so they may move on in their journey to serve You. There is nothing left in this area: no job, children, or other family members that is holding them back. A new and exciting future is calling out to them, and the only thing holding them back is the sale of their home. Please allow the right person to be overwhelmed by the beauty of this house that has been a home. Allow this same person to find they must buy this house and make it their home or a home for a beloved one of their own. I request for my family/friends that an offer is made on the house for the amount asked. I ask that the offer is accepted, the inspector finds the home in perfect working order, and the closing is effortless and within thirty days of the offer being accepted. I give thanks that this is for everyone's greatest and highest good. I see the property SOLD!

So it is!

Simple Prayer for Sale of Inherited Property

Dearest _____,

I give thanks for your presence in my life and the presence You have in my friend's/family's life. My friends/family inherited homes and property. A bittersweet blessing of its own, the inheritance of the property has created an overabundance of complications surrounding the ownership of these homes. My friends/family would like to simplify their lives. _____ could use the cash flow and freedom from the emotional baggage that came with inheriting after the loss of a loved one. The quick sale of the properties would allow for more mobility in their time and money. I ask that _____ release the sentimental value of the properties so they may move on in their lives. I ask that the sale of these properties be swift and complete. I ask that offers on the properties for the amount asked and the closings happen within thirty days of the acceptance of the offer. I ask that the inspection and closings go without any complications and that my friends have enough time to clear out personal items without causing undue stress on all involved.

I give thanks that my prayer has been heard. I see the properties as being SOLD!

So it is! ***Editor's note: At this point in editing, I was intrigued by this particular prayer. My daughter recently inherited a property up north and was anxious to sell it before winter. I decided I had nothing to lose by concentrating on this prayer, so I proceeded to light a candle and focus on the power of the words. Within four hours, she received an offer on the house. Although the first offer came in very low, within 24 hours she had an offer that she could not refuse. The property has now sold for more than she was asking and met all of the terms she was hoping for. These prayers are very powerful! Peggy RavenWolf

FINDING A JOB AND A PLACE TO LIVE

Two of my friends have just had the toughest of times figuring out where they need to be living and finding a job. Both are in their 60s and are very good at what they want to do. Both lost or walked away from jobs due to either the economy or politics in the workplace. It was painful watching them pack everything they owned to head to another state for the promise of something greater, but to head back to the state they really wanted to live there within a year. One had the possibility of a job, but the other was just floundering. The irony is they both left the same state, moved to the same state, and went back to the first state at about the same time. They only knew each other by name and through associations connected through me. Every time they attempted to meet, the universe sent one or the other on some rabbit trail that had to be explored at that moment. This prayer is for my wandering and confused friends.

Prayer for Guidance and Clarity

Dearest Creator,

I am grateful that You are in my life and part of my life. I am grateful for my Guides and Angels and for Kara and Kimberly's Guides and Angels. I am grateful that Kara and Kimberly are in my life. Creator, my beloved friends are floundering like a fish out of the water. They both believe they are following your guidance. I ask that You make your guidance a bit clearer for both.

So it is!

Prayer for a Vocation

Dearest Creator,

My prayer for Kara, now that she has figured out where she needs to be living, is that it is time for her to find the perfect job. We are asking for a job that is her passion. As an intensive care nurse, we are looking for a private care position either as a live in with private quarters or in a position that runs four days a week. We request her charges be children with special needs. We request the parents be open to Kara's suggestions in the care of the child. We request whatever position Kara acquires, she is loved, respected, and compensated appropriately. We ask that this issue be settled quickly so she may calmly prepare herself for your service with this infant/special needs child that she will be in charge of. There is no greater service than the care of a child, unless it is the care of a child with special needs. Lord, please pair my special friend with her special family and child. Kara and I accept this as a reality and give thanks.

So it is!

Prayer for a Home and a Job

Dearest Creator,

I give thanks for, You, Creator, for your presence in my life and my friend Kimberly's life. Kimberly has been running around attempting to find a job for several months now. Until recently, not finding gainful employment has been more annoying than necessary. The jobs she did find were not a good fit. Promises were made and not kept; integrity seemed to be missing in the management. Now, Creator, we are asking that Kimberly find a position in the state she is currently residing in. This job needs to be part time, 20 to 30 hours a week, with three concurrent days off every week. Preferably, one of the days is a weekend day. Kimberly loves sales; we are asking this to be a sales job. Her base pay and salary combined will allow Kimberly to have extra money to visit her children and grandchildren with the freedom to spend money on both. Creator, Kimberly is a positive, bubbly, fun-loving individual. Everyone who works or plays with Kimberly is impressed with her joyous sincerity. There is a perfect job close to where she is living now that is just waiting for her. A job where the customers love her and the management recognizes and respects her incredible sales ability. I see it! Kimberly is now willing to stop wandering across the universe looking for something that is in her own backyard. Please open her eyes to what this job is. Open the doors so she may walk in and accept the position she deserves with the compensation, love, and respect she deserves.

So it is!

Simple Prayer for Someone to Find Work

Dearest _____

I give thanks for You, and that You are in my life and in the life of my friend. _____, I am praying for my friend. She/he is bereft and needs help in finding a good position within a company that respects her/his knowledge, loves her/his attitude, and is willing to compensate with appropriate money and time off. I pray a position is found now. Through you, all is possible. I turn this over to You.

In _____ name, so it is!

FINDING A HOME

Along with not having a job, neither friend has a permanent place to stay. Both of my friends are watching someone else's place while the owners of the home are playing in other countries. Very strange the parallel lives these two women are living. My next prayer will encompass both of them.

Prayer for Finding a Home

Dearest Creator,

I give thanks for You and my Guides and Angels. I give thanks for Kara and Kimberly and their Guides and Angels. Creator, I give thanks as both women have given thanks that You found them temporary housing while they are in flux. I pray that Kara and Kimberly will find a permanent base to call home by the time the homeowners come back from their trips. I ask that these homes are big enough that their children and grandchildren may visit. The emphasis here is visit! I ask, Creator, that these domiciles are within their budget and in the area of their newly found jobs. I ask that the homes are beautiful, aesthetically pleasing, and have all the necessary appliances. They should also be in a safe neighborhood.

I give thanks that their Angels are already helping both ladies manifest what they need and desire.

So it is!

This prayer has some options in parentheses. Not everyone wants woods or gardens. Some people need furniture and some need turnkey. A younger couple or a single mother/father may need a place to raise children; others need a place for their pets. Substitute where you need to. Pray for exactly what is needed and wanted. Be specific! I am writing this as if I am writing it for someone. With some modifications, it can easily be for you. Specify a range of what you think you or the person you are praying for can afford.

Simple Prayer for Finding a Perfect Home

Dearest _____,

I give thanks for You and my Guides and Angels. I am praying today for _____. They are currently in need of a place to call home. (Some Need a place to raise children, a temporary place, a permanent place, a place that will accept pets.) This place needs to be in a safe neighborhood. It needs to be (furnished, unfurnished, yard or no yard, wooded or not wooded). It needs to be close to work and must be within budget $_____. I know that there is a place that is perfect for _____ that meets these criteria. I give thanks and now turn this over to You.

So it is!

TRAVELING

In life, traveling is probably one of my favorite things to do. Flying, driving, or floating anywhere is a passion of mine. I also love coming home. My prayer for traveling has something that not everyone would agree with. I call it folding time. Sometimes it works, which makes the journey even more interesting. The simplified prayer will not have time folding in it.

Prayer for Traveling

Dearest Creator,

I give thanks for You and my Guides and Angels. Creator, I am on another journey. I so love journeys! I love getting in my car and meeting new people, some new friends, and some old friends and family. I love exploring new areas and having You divinely guide me to the people and places that will make a difference in their lives and mine.

I ask, Creator, that You have my Guardian Angel wrap his wings around my vehicle and me. I ask that You protect me/us, my vehicle from all animate, inanimate objects, all bugs, animals, and humans. I ask that You protect all animate, inanimate objects, bugs, and humans from me and my vehicle. I ask that You keep those I leave behind: my family, pets, friends, business, and home all under your protection.

I ask, Creator, that my vehicle is roadworthy. I ask that the brakes work perfectly, the engine purrs, and the tires, lights, and wipers work just as they were made to work. God, if You see fit, I would also like to fold time. I would like to reach my destination in a timely manner without speeding and with plenty of time to stop and meet whomever I need to meet.

I ask that You fill this journey with joy, laughter, love, and education. I give thanks as your servant, Creator, for this is going to be an awesome journey.

So it is!

FLYING

I think flying has become my second favorite way of travel. It used to be my first choice. The coolest thing happens when I do a prayer for any vehicle that I am in. An awesome display of emerald green and royal purple aura surrounds the vehicle. The Angels show themselves in colors so I may relax and enjoy my journey. I really appreciate this show of protection when I am flying.

Simple Travel Prayer

Dearest _____,

I give thanks for this opportunity to travel. I/we ask _____ that my vehicle is road worthy. I ask that the brakes work perfectly, the engine purrs, and the tires, lights, and wipers work just as they were made to work. I ask that You direct me to talk to those whom I need to talk with, that I see what I need to, and that I learn what I need accomplish. I ask that You keep those I leave behind: my family, pets, friends, business, and home all under your protection. I give thanks for this awesome opportunity.

So it is!

Simple Prayer for Flying

Dearest _____,

I give thanks for this opportunity to fly to _____. I give thanks to my Guides and Angels. In particular, I give thanks for my Guardian Angels and for Archangel Michael. I ask that You have the Angels wrap their protective wings around this plane. I ask that You help our pilot and his crew be the best that they can be today. I ask that inclement weather does not affect us. I ask that we safely take off and land. I ask that You sit me next to someone who is awesome and that the children on this flight sleep or giggle throughout the journey.

I give thanks that all of this is possible. So it is!

*Only the Glory of God exceeds the
Glory of Mother Earth.*

EARTH AND ALL OUR RELATIONS

MOTHER EARTH

This prayer may bother some of my more fundamental readers. It comes from my heart and soul. If you have problems with how I start or end the prayer or if the heart of the prayer goes against your beliefs, just skip it.

Several years ago, I went on a vision quest. I spent thirty-six hours without food or water on Black Mountain in North Carolina. Pretty amazing, especially considering I was diabetic and did not know it. I was scheduled as a helper, not a quester! The story about this will be found in one of my future books. On my way back to Florida, the friend I was traveling with suggested we take the long way home. Susie decided she wanted to mine crystals in Arkansas. I had nowhere to be, and it sounded like an excellent idea. At the time, my licensed massage establishment also had a rock shop and a bookstore. Accumulating free or inexpensive crystals was and still is worth a rabbit trail. The trip turned out not to be a rabbit trail.

The night we landed on Mt. Ida, Arkansas, I had a dream that was so powerful and so meaningful it almost overshadowed my vision quest.

In my dream, I was sitting around an outdoor fire pit burning pine logs. Tall pine trees stood a few yards away and a cliff was close by overlooking a valley with a river, homes, and several industries including a nuclear power plant. An amazing woman approached me, beautiful in ways that some would find terrifying. I was in awe! She was Mother Earth! She had eyes that would change from a deep sea green to the deepest sky blue. Then, as she talked to me, they became stormy grey to jet-black with stars reflecting in them. I had to ignore the morphs that were happening while she talked to me in order to pay attention to what she wanted me to do and why. Her face, hair, body, and clothes kept changing as she expressed her love for her wards, her anger and fear as to what we humans were doing to her. Each emotion shifted her appearance. I had a difficult time focusing.

Mother Earth, Gaia (one of the names of earth), asked in my dream, "Before you take one crystal, I ask that you do a healing prayer for the area and then for the whole planet and my wards." Mother also stated we could take what we could carry, but when she gave the signal, the warning, we were to immediately finish and go. The next morning I told my friend Suzie what was required. What follows is my prayer for Mother Earth and as the Native Americans would say, "All our Relations."

Prayer for Mother Earth, Gaia

Creator, Mother, Father, God,

I give thanks for You, Creator, for my Guides and Angels. I give thanks for Mother Earth and for my friend who is here with me to share this wonderful experience. I sit in silence as I absorb the beauty around me. I hear the raven caw in the distance. As I breathe in the scent of pine, I watch two startled deer leap in front of me. I smile as they stop almost in mid-leap to stare at me before bounding away. They were not fearful, only on their way to something not involving humans. I watch the ground squirrels, busy being squirrels. I feel joy. As I look closer and become more aware, I now see what Mother Earth had warned me about. Many of the trees are brittle and brown, and there are other signs of destruction.

Creator, I ask that You bless this ground that I am walking on. I pray for squirrels, deer, birds, and other wild beasts. I pray for the water and the earth that somehow You keep them safe from us and our ignorance. Please, God, help us understand that we must take care of our planet, the four legged ones, the winged ones, the creepy crawly ones, the plants, our water, and our air. They are our relations. Please help us wake up before it is too late.

AH-Ho!

Simple Prayer for Our Planet

I give thanks for You,

I give thanks for this beautiful planet that you have allowed me to live on. I give thanks for clean water, clean air, beautiful trees, and all the many animals. I am in awe of the beauty that surrounds me. I pray for our planet as she is going through much upheaval. Colossal storms, tsunamis, earthquakes, fires, droughts, landslides, blizzards, hail, floods, and tornadoes. I understand that all of these are the nature of our planet. I pray that the events that are being brought on by our own ignorance and greed and not by nature itself, stop. Please wake up those who would kill the last animal of its species just for the sake of killing. Please wake up the manufacturers who think it is alright to put toxins in our air, water, and food. Please help my species wake up before it is too late. I give thanks for your presence in my life.

So it is!

WEATHER

Florida is a state that has some of the best weather in the world and then it does not. Living in Florida is like the poem of the little girl with the curl in her hair. When she is good she is very, very good, and when she is bad she's horrid.

I love Florida most of the time. I came from a state that had tornadoes all the time. While I was away from home, my house in Illinois was hit twice with minor damage. Living in Illinois, not once did I get to see a tornado! Since moving to Florida, I have seen dozens of waterspouts and small twisters. I have lived through some of the most frightening storms. Living all the way down on the West Coast does not give much room to run if it gets really ugly!

Prayer for Those in a Storm's Path

Dearest Creator,

It looks as if we have a storm coming our way. I know that is the earth's way to cleanse the planet. I understand that this is nature's plan, and I am praying that this storm diminish in its power and that it not be as destructive as our weathermen say it might be. I ask, Creator that You watch over the animals that have nowhere to hide during the storm. I ask that You keep my family, friends, and our properties and businesses safe. I give thanks that You are watching over me and my circle of family and friends.

So it is!

Simple Prayer for Those in a Storm's Path

Dearest _____,

It looks as if we have a storm coming our way. I know that is the earth's way to cleanse the planet. I understand that this is nature's plan, and I am praying that this storm diminishes in its power and that it not be as destructive as our weathermen say it might be. I ask that You watch over the animals that have nowhere to hide during the storm. I ask that You keep my family, friends, and our properties and businesses safe. I give thanks that You are watching over me and my circle of family and friends.

So it is!

CLEANUP AND INTEGRITY

Dearest Creator,

I give thanks that You watched over my friends and family during the storm. We sustained some damage in our businesses and our homes; fortunately all the damages are fixable. Creator, I ask that You help my community piece itself back together. I give thanks that the loss of life was less than expected and the damage in the community can be repaired. I send out prayers for healing and peace of mind for those who lost lives or property. I give thanks that You are giving us the strength and courage to rebuild and persevere. I give thanks for your guidance and strength. Through You all things are possible.

So it is!

Simple Prayer for Cleanup and Integrity

Dearest _____,

I give thanks that You watched over my friends and family during the storm. We sustained some minor damages in our businesses; fortunately, damages are fixable. I ask that You help my community piece itself back together. I give thanks that the loss of life was less than expected and the damage in the community can be repaired. I send out prayers for healing and peace of mind for those who lost lives or property. I give thanks that You are giving us the strength and courage to rebuild and persevere. I give thanks for charitable help groups who have provided aid and shelter for those in need. I ask that the insurance companies treat their customers fairly and with compassion. I give thanks for the rules that are in place to help those who have suffered. I give thanks for your guidance and strength.

Through You, all things are possible. So it is.

OCEANS, LAKES, RIVERS, FOREST, PRAIRIES, AND THEIR INHABITANTS

Being empathic has always been a difficult road for me. I feel things deep in my soul: joy, sorrow, and physical pain. I have to be careful what I watch, read, or listen to. If I see an animal hurt by a human, immediately I get unreasonably angry. If at all possible, I will put myself between them and the animal. (I am the same way with children and battered women.) It is my nature, and it sickens me when someone talks of slaughtering dolphins, whales, or any animal. It sickens me to know that animals suffer every day in laboratories. At this time, all I can do is pray for them and their souls. I know many people don't believe animals have souls, but I beg to differ. If a being is capable of loving, there must be a soul. (My own personal opinion!)

We humans believe it is our right to toss cigarette butts on the ground, not caring if the grass or forest is dry. Our rights are more important, or so we think! We think it is okay to kill off whales and dolphins and that wolves, bears and large cats have no right to live in their habitats that we have taken over. It angers me. If my mate wants to aggravate me, he puts on the hunter's channel and leaves it on just long enough for the kill. I have many hunters in my family. I have eaten at their tables, given thanks, and prayed for the life of the animal I was eating. I am not a hypocrite as some might call me. I am empathic, and I feel for all beings. I am working on being a vegetarian, so far I have not succeeded in giving up meat.

We humans have done horrible things to our planet; prairies are now cities and houses. Ancient forests are now buildings, furniture, and paper. Our waterways are filled with garbage, sewage, and toxic waste. Our oceans are filled with trash and radioactive waste. Wildlife has been depleted, in many cases, to extinction.

I can do my part to the best of my ability, and I can pray.

Prayer for Oceans, Lakes, Rivers, Forest, Prairies, and Their Inhabitants

Dearest Creator,

    I give thanks for your presence in my life and for the presence of my Guides and Angels. Creator, my heart is both heavy and full today. I am sitting in a beautiful wooded area and basking in the nature of the day. I have watched a doe graze on the grass as her young fawn suckled. It gave me joy and peace. I have watched a murder of crows work with a young crow as a team, showing the youth what it needed to know. It was a glorious morning. I thank You for all of the wood's beauty and peace.

    I hear chainsaws in the distance and am reminded of the acres of forest that are being torn down for a new housing development. I wonder, do we really need a new development? Where will the deer, fox, and wildcats go?

    I live in Florida where there are many environmental lawsuits fighting the damages that our government and oil companies have caused. Record numbers of dolphin, manatee, and fish have washed up onto the shore in the last few years. Our estuaries have been damaged or destroyed. There is a huge wasteland at the bottom of the gulf where nothing lives. We have new developments going up every day, primarily for humans' second and third homes. Lord, please help us not be so greedy, not be so callus and narcissistic. Please help us temper our desires for more before it is too late. Help us use our resources in an appropriate manner.

    Bless the natural inhabitants of our prairies, forests, mountains, air, oceans, lakes, rivers, and streams.

    I give thanks for the beauty that surrounds me. I give thanks for the planet and all her glory. So it is!

Simple Prayer Oceans, Lakes, Rivers, Forests, Prairies and Their Inhabitants

Dearest _____,

What a blessing this day is. I give thanks for the beauty of nature that surrounds me. I give thanks for the fresh air and the vivid colors of the grass and the trees. I give thanks for the wildlife that I sense or see. I give thanks for the beauty of the lakes, rivers, and oceans. I give thanks for all the wildlife that lives on our planet.

Please help us not be so greedy, not be so callus and narcissistic. Please help us temper our desires for more before it is too late. Help us use our resources in an appropriate manner.

Bless the natural inhabitants of our prairies, forests, mountains, air, oceans, lakes, rivers, and streams.

I give thanks for the beauty that surrounds me. I give thanks for the planet and all her glory. So it is!

Even in flight, we are told to put on our oxygen mask before helping others. You must take care of yourself in order to help others. Do not feel selfish when praying for yourself.

PRAYERS FOR YOURSELF

PRAYERS FOR SELF

We have a tendency to pray for others and forget to pray for ourselves. I don't mean the beseeching prayer. I am talking about the prayer when we have reached a point that it feels the world has fallen around us and there is no hope. I talk to God and my Angels daily. I pray for others all day. I'm so busy taking care of others that unless I have a particular need, I forget my own needs. Many of us reading this book are the same way. We worry about others until all of a sudden something horrific or beyond comprehension happens to ourselves. I am not a fundamentalist, and I believe in Jesus. I believe in Jesus Christ and a loving God.

I had health issues that were not clearing up. In fact, the medical system had me terrified. I was not frightened of death. I have died and lived to tell many stories about those times. The medical system had me in a quandary about how much pain I was going to have to endure over the next couple months to possibly years.

I went out to dinner one night, and a church group held hands and prayed before they ate. After they prayed, I walked over and introduced myself. I should not have been surprised when I was told I addressed God wrong. My prayer should only be addressed to Jesus Christ my Savior. I was asking for help. Instead of being helped, I was judged. Possibly they did pray for me. Later that evening, I called friends and asked to be put on as many prayer lists as they could connect me with. My healing began. I move toward my new life paths; the pain eases. I'm hearing You, my beloved Creator. With all the signs You have sent me, I also realize You are hearing me.

Sometimes, health issues turn out to be a statement from God that it's time to change something in your life.

Self Prayer

Dearest Creator,

Somehow, I have gotten lost again. It started again when three of my closest friends made their passage to You. I miss them and know they are with You. Then my mate was in a terrible auto accident. I kept my faith. Then somehow I ruptured a cyst on my kidneys and two disks in my back. For twenty years, I have facilitated healing through massage, Reiki, and prayer. I am beginning to question my faith. Forty-five procedures, tests, surgeries, and doctor's appointments in less than six weeks over two holidays where my family had all left the area or passed away. I have felt abandoned. I fell down on my knees and asked for help. I asked for an answer and for the strength to follow your orders and guidance. I cried more tears than my pillows could hold. You listened. I give thanks for someone suggesting I open my own book, make the corrections, and move forward. I ask,God, that You continue to guide me. I ask that the pain be eased so I may fulfill my commitments and start on my new adventures. I give thanks for You. I know You will show me the path and the way. And, eventually, the pain will diminish.

Thank You, God. So it is.

Simple Prayer for Self

Dearest _____,

I have lost my way and am beginning to question my faith. I am asking for a sign that You are still there. I am asking to be shown my way and direction. I am asking for the strength to follow through on what I need to accomplish. I know You put me here for a reason. I give thanks for life. In _____, so it is.

My Favorite Prayer

I give thanks for You,

Creator, my Guides and Angels. I give thanks for peace of mind, love, joy, prosperity, and good health. I give thanks that I am your servant and as your servant, I am worthy.

So it is!

PRAY WITHOUT CEASING

The book *Prayer, When You Don't Have the Words* ends and prayer continues. Learning to pray and believing you are worthy for God to answer your prayer takes practice and repetition. If you need to beseech, don't make the whole prayer about your dire need. Take a breath and give thanks for God's presence in your life. Prayer is not just for bedtime, meals, and funerals. Prayer needs to become the second waking thought, if not the first and last thought of the day.

Life becomes easier the more you pray with giving thanks for the blessings you have.

HOW I CAME TO BELIEVE

I SEE ANGELS, AND I WALKED WITH JESUS

I see angels. I have walked with Jesus. My life has not been easy. Almost everything dark and painful known to man that could happen, has happened to my family members, my close friends, or to myself. I wondered, "Why me?" I have heard, "Why not you?" I am told that I am a vessel for healing the body, mind, spirit, and soul. I was three years old when I shared my first Holy Spirit experience with my Mother, who had an intense belief in God, although she did not attend church.

My Parents and Grandmother Dobbs

Let me begin by telling you about my parents and Grandmother Dobbs. My parents were damaged goods. They were saints and sinners. The reader will often be in conflict when I talk about the good, bad, ugliness, and beauty of these people who brought me into this world. I remember both sides so clearly. Dad would give you the shirt off his back if you needed it, but if anyone upset him, he took his anger out on me—a frail, small strawberry blond toddler—with the back of his hand. He was five foot ten, two hundred and forty pounds of muscle with auburn hair and hazel eyes. He was brilliant. His IQ was over 160. He believed in God in his own way. When we moved to his mother's house in Gainesville, Georgia, he began physically abusing me. I was almost three. He stopped backhanding me when I was about seven, almost two years after we moved to Illinois.

Dad

Dad enlisted in the Army when he was seventeen years old as a paratrooper. The year was 1944. He was running away from an incestuous situation. His mother had abused him from the time he was five until he escaped to the Army. *It is now known that those who are abused sometimes become abusers.* I found my father's original service records after my father had passed on, which showed he had experienced five tours of duty. When I requested his "official" records from St Louis, I was sent a transcript saying he had only served six months and was honorably discharged. However, transcripts that I had found in an old box had all of his five tours of duty, and for the last tour, there were no discharge papers. There remain some mysteries concerning my father's military service.

Dad married a young, appropriate southern Christian woman, and they had a handsome son. This was a woman whom his mother chose and approved of. After the second or third tour of duty, my father never saw his wife again. He saw his son one other time. When my father was overseas, he became involved with a young Japanese woman. She was a virgin and twelve years old. She had been given to him to "deflower." *I just recently found out that when he came home on leave, he brought the young pregnant woman (Katie) with him to the States. He had hoped to set up house with his wife, son, and Katie. Offended, the proper southern wife did not agree to this arrangement; Katie supposedly died in childbirth.* With all the lies I had been told over the years, Katie's death may be a big one. I may have a half sibling that knows nothing of me, and I know nothing of them. The request to bring his child concubine into his home opened his family's eyes that my father had an unhealthy interest in pre-adolescent girls. One of my half-sisters was the first in our family to find this out. She was twelve.

Mother

My mother was beautiful. She was five feet five and a perfect size eight. She had long auburn hair, intense sky blue eyes, full lips, large breasts, and a small waist and hips. I was her fifth child. She looked as if she had never had children. Mother had the voice of an angel. Barbra Streisand would have been jealous if they had to compete with each

Prayer When You Don't Have the Words

other. She was almost thirty nine when she had me. Whenever she could, she wore hot pants, short skirts, tight pants—any clothing that would show off her curves and her incredible legs. She knew she had the power to turn heads. Still, she had so little confidence in spite of a huge ego.

Mother quit school in her junior year of high school. She didn't smile much because her front teeth had been knocked out by a bully at a drinking fountain. Thank God for the dentist. As an adult, she had the teeth fixed. *She had the most beautiful smile.* Mother had been assaulted in every way you could think of as a child. She wet the bed even after she married her first husband. Mom's first husband wasn't any kinder to her than her parents had been.

She fell in love with a man who looked like Robert Taylor, the actor. *For my family's sake I'm going to call her ex-husband Bill from here on out.* Bill was in the service. Mother became pregnant her junior year of high school. She believed she should marry the man who made her pregnant. Bill dragged her off to have an abortion in the back room of a seedy hotel when she was four months along. Mother still married him. She had four more children by him. Bill got drunk and took a gun to her head the night she left him. The gun misfired. This was the second time he had taken a gun to her head, and it misfired again. She decided not to take the chance that there would be a third incident. Mother figured she wouldn't be so lucky. He passed out. It was payday, and she found his check, gathered some basic things and left in the middle of the night with four children, ages six to fourteen. They ran from Illinois to California. Mother was thirty four. She had friends in California, and they gave her and my half siblings a place to stay. Mother would meet a number of men in California. Two of the men would be important in the formation of my life. One of those men, age 34, had sexually exploited my then 15 year old sister. He was married to another woman at the time the first pregnancy happened. Their first child died within nine months while my sister was pregnant with their second child. He then divorced his wife and married my sister. This same man had dated my mother for a short time. My mother was responsible for their meeting. My mother would attempt to set up each one of her daughters, including me, with a man that was not appropriate. The second man that was important in the formation of my life, would become my father; he was twenty nine. Dad conned his way into my mother's life.

My mother was the perfect victim and my father the perfect predator. Both loved and wanted to be loved. Neither parent knew how to love appropriately. What I am sharing is not the tip of the iceberg... it is just a few snow flurries from the hell my life was at times. I have been asked how I survived living with two sick souls.

My parents changed. God put me in my family for a reason. I learned to love the monsters. I learned to look deeper into a person's soul before I judged. I learned to feel their pain and release it. I learned that I needed to have clear and protective boundaries.

I learned about the Angels and Jesus. I learned to trust God.

Grandmother Dobbs

My mother told me my grandmother on my father's side was not a good person. In her own sick way she loved her son. Grandmother Dobbs came to love me and tolerated my mother. My father served two prison sentences, one while he was in the service. *There is no paperwork to support this, and my mother and my oldest sister insisted the story was true.* The other prison time was for kiting checks. As the stories were told to me, both prison terms were reversed or expunged.

I was almost two when he went to prison the second time. When he was released, he was told he had to leave California and never come back. Grandmother Dobbs insisted we move to Georgia where she lived. My grandmother knew something we did not know at the time. My father was still legally married to his first wife when he married my mother. *We found out about this little gem several years after my father had passed on.* Grandmother Dobbs treated my mother like a servant. Most of my memories of my mother in Georgia consisted of seeing her scrubbing the floor on her hands and knees, standing over a hot stove cooking or polishing tons of silver. My father was always angry during the time we lived with his mother. His anger at Grandmother Dobbs would result in the first two of the head injuries I would suffer over my lifetime. By the time I was three, I knew much more than a child should ever know about life. I learned to hide when the adults were arguing.

In those days, all the adults in my family smoked cigarettes, except for my Grandmother Dobbs, who chewed tobacco. There was always one or two lit cigarettes in an ashtray and at least one dangling from someone's mouth. Four to six packs a day were being filtered by my little lungs. They called me a sickly child. One day, my father and I both came down with pneumonia. Dad was treated by a doctor, and he was able to go to work. Grandmother Dobbs refused to let the doctor see me since she was paying the bill.

My spiritual journey started that day.

THE MAN IN THE WHITE DRESS: MY FIRST ANGELIC EXPERIENCE

On this particular day, my temperature spiked a hundred and five degrees. I had pneumonia. We had no money for a doctor, and my mother was alone with me. She filled the bathtub with what felt like ice water and made me stay in the tub for what seemed like hours. Of course it was not ice water and it was not hours; it was minutes. She was scared. *I was the last of five living children, and there was ten to twenty years between myself and my half siblings. I was the child that wasn't supposed to be. My mother had me at the advanced age of thirty eight, just weeks before her thirty ninth birthday... My parents were going through a divorce when she found out that she was pregnant with me. Both Mom and Dad told me that when she found out she was pregnant, she drank a gallon of vodka to kill herself and the baby within her. My father forcefully stuck his fingers down her throat and made her throw up. She did not love me until the moment she saw me in the hospital. She said it was love at first sight. I was born on her mother's, my Grandmother Master's, birthday.*

After the bath, mother bundled me up and tucked me into bed. She was exhausted and fell asleep cuddling with me. I am not sure how much time passed before I heard a man's voice calling me, not by my nickname. He called me by my given name: "Tamara, Tamara, Tamara, come to me."

I got out of bed without waking my mother; I followed the voice. The man's voice came from the kitchen. The red brick house was small, and it was cold. The front bedroom, where she and I had been sleeping, and the only bathroom were as far away from the kitchen as any room could be. The voice was in my head, and it kept repeating, "Come to me, Tamara." I turned the corner into the kitchen, and a man all in white was floating in the left corner of the room. He wanted me to go with him. I asked to stay. He granted my wish.

I was tired and cold after our encounter. I padded back down the hallway and went to the warmest place in the house. The bathroom sink was partially blocking a heater vent. We always had heated towels after a bath because they kept the towels under the sink. I crawled under the sink and into the towels. I left my tiny little foot out of my warm space in the cabinet.

My mother woke up and discovered I was not in the bed, and within minutes, she found I was in no logical place in the house. She began screaming for me. I started to wake and moved my leg, and she saw the door to the sink cabinet move, and then she saw my foot. She yanked me out of the sink cabinet abruptly, which of course made me cry. She was still scared and still yelling until she realized I was okay. My temperature had broken, and I was breathing normally. Once she calmed both of us down, the questions started.

"Why did you get out of bed?"

"A man called me and asked me to go with him."

"What man?!"

"The man in the kitchen."

My mother was bewildered and even more scared. "Show me where the man was in the kitchen."

With my tiny little hand, I grabbed two of her fingers and led her to the kitchen. With the other hand I pointed up towards the ceiling in the left corner of the room.

She kneeled down, grabbed my face and studied my demeanor and reactions. Still with fear in her eyes, she asked me in a quiet voice, 'What did he look like?"

"He was all dressed in white, he had white hair, and he had a white beard."

"Were you afraid?"

"No."

"What did he want?"

"He wanted to take *me* out of my body."

She was now having a hard time controlling her emotions. She repeated, "You weren't afraid?" *My mother knew I had a fear of bearded men. I couldn't even stand Santa Claus at that time of my life.*

'No, I was not afraid. I liked him."

"Why did you not go?" Talking over me she asked before I responded.

"I asked to stay with you, Bryce, and Gram." *I did not mention my Grandmother Dobbs or my father.*

That was my first manifestation of an Angel. It was not the last.

After this Angelic experience, I began to ask questions. I heard adult conversations about God, Angels, and Jesus. I wanted to know who Jesus was. Who were these "imaginary" friends who protected me, and did God really sit on a pedestal of Gold? I begged to go to church. Over the next few years, I went to any church any adult would take me to, and as I became more independent, I walked to all the churches in our community.

My Father told me that before he joined the army, he had planned to become a Methodist minister. My mother introduced my father to a non-denominational church. He did eventually become a deacon of The Science of Mind Church in Peoria. (This is not to be confused with Scientology or Christian Science, it is closer to Unity, a non-denominational church.) My mother had her own beliefs that veered off the beaten path. She was also a spiritual healer. Before meeting my father, she had attended the Science of Mind Church in Los Angeles.

As I mentioned in other parts of this book, my parents were incredible people with some horrible addictions. Those who know my story have wondered how I survived my parents. My parents truly loved me to the best of their abilities, and I also believe I survived because my parents found their way back to believing in and loving God.

HEAD ON WITH A MACK TRUCK

December 11, 1985

I was living in Morton, Illinois, and I was a teller in a small community bank in East Peoria. Work was slow that dreary cold December day. My mother and I had plans to go Christmas shopping, have dinner and then to play bingo that evening. My boss suggested that I go home early. She did not have to ask me twice. I called my mother and let her know we could start early. I would be home in 15 minutes, I would change my clothes, and off we would go. She and I were getting along very well at that time. When I arrived at our brick ranch style home, Mother was out of character. Her mood did not seem to fit mine. She was not excited that we were going to do fun things for ourselves and others. Christmas was always her favorite holiday; her attitude should have been joyful. She was quiet and reflective, there was a heaviness in her energy. I was about to learn why...

I'm going to throw in a back story that really sets this event up.

In March, of the same year, my dad woke up screaming. "Hep me. Hep me! Something is wrong!" *My father never had a southern accent unless he was talking about light "bubs" or "hep."* He was southern at heart, and he could not say help or bulbs without an accent. His fear was strong and real. I called the police for help. We did not have 911 in our area at that time.

He had experienced a severe stroke. For most of eight months after the cerebral event, he was either in intensive care or a rehab center. The stroke affected the center of his brain. We were told that he would probably be wheelchair bound, and he may not be able to speak. There was really nothing they (the hospital) could do for him. While my mother was crying and begging my dad to survive, I had an epiphany. If Dad survived, he was going to be impossible to live with.

His Sybil attitude and demeanor were already difficult to tolerate. He was brilliant (160+ IQ), and he was awesome, and he was horrible in ways that in today's society would have put him in prison. However, back in the 1980's, my family (women and children) did not have a voice. Whatever the man of the house did was accepted. If you were a sensitive child like me, you loved unconditionally. I loved people, even the monsters. I felt Dad was going to be a big problem. I told my mother this, and she said she didn't care. She wanted her Chris back. So we prayed.

Over the next several months, my dad had dozens of grand mal seizures. He repeatedly ripped out any tubing he had, and he talked to people we could not see or hear. When he could talk, he told a story that while on the other side he was met with a panel of twelve men. They told him that there was something he had to correct here in this life before he could go home to God. When Dad came home from the hospital and rehabilitation center, he was extremely angry that he could not do the things he loved to do. He was paralyzed on the right side of his body. He had to learn to write with his left hand, and his walking was limited. His mouth drooped and sometimes he drooled. He had been a good looking man (he looked a lot like Hemingway), and he still was good looking; however, eating with him was unpleasant.

People with head injuries, as I would learn first-hand, sometimes have poor behavior and can be very angry for no apparent reason. My father, who would backhand me because he wanted to lash out at someone before the stroke, was now having to be served and waited on. He was so emotionally and psychologically abusive to my mother that she could no longer bear it. This brings us back to December 11,1985.

I can be a chatterbox, especially when I am excited. I was twenty-five when the accident occurred. I got off work early, and I was going to hang out with my best friend, my mother. I felt something was not right. I have been empathic and intuitive since my first near death experience. I got quiet to match her quietness. We had not even pulled completely out of the driveway.

"What's wrong?"

Mother hemmed and hawed a moment, and then she said, "What I am going to tell you, you can't tell anyone! And then you will be as guilty as I am!"

I thought, "What the heck did she do now?" I knew both of them had kited checks once in a while and were not in their total integrity. Both had affairs. Hmmm... I thought, "What could she possibly say that would surprise me or make me guilty of anything?" I had a wild side when I was younger, mostly to keep my sanity, and at this particular moment, I was good with God. I spent a lot of time talking to God, and my heart was filled with love for the two misguided souls called my parents. I had the judgments under control.

My best friend, my mother, said, "I'm murdering your father!"

I looked at her and exclaimed, "UH... WHAT?!"

"I can't stand it anymore, and now that you're sworn to secrecy, you are just as guilty as I am!"

I looked away; we had turned on to I-55. A few hundred yards away was a bridge that had railroad tracks about six stories down. An Ice storm had come out of nowhere. The tires were not new. Disaster was in the making. I had *not* been sworn to secrecy as she claimed. I would *not* let this happen. "God, I need some help here!" I said in my head.

I heard in my head, "Ask your mother when and how."

"How are you going to do this?" I asked as I tried not to hyperventilate.

"I am poisoning him with his own medications. I changed them out," was her reply.

My mother was courageous in many ways and in others she was not. I knew this was not going to happen. She was telling me because—thank God!—she could be a wuss. I questioned, "When did you start messing with his medicine?"

"Today," she stated.

"Thank God!" was my first internal response, followed by a desperate talk with God.

"God, you and I both know she has done no harm yet. I know how to combat this. When I get home tonight, I will fix my father's medicine box, and tomorrow I will get my mother the psychiatric help she needs... If I seem displeased or react in a way that offends her, this will not go well."

At the very moment I was talking to God, my mother screamed," OH MY GOD!"

I put my hand up in a protective reaction as a Mack truck filled with Caterpillar parts hit us left of center head on. To this day, I don't know if she drove intentionally into the truck or if she had no choice between hitting the vehicle or flying off the bridge down to the railroad tracks. And this is where the Angels came in...

ANGELS

The story that happened next has several parts. Some people who are still alive may have some minor differences and slightly different stories. How big the truck was, who was or wasn't on the rescue team, was I or wasn't I put to the side of the icy road and covered with a blanket. I was told I had no vitals. I know I was no longer in my body. I can only share what I had been told later about those other facts. My story about our time on the other side never changed and neither did my mother's.

We were in the ICU, two or three rooms down from each other, not long after being admitted. The timing could have been hours or a day.

Mother's Interpretation of the Events as She Told Them to Me

We were just entering the bridge when I looked over to tell Tammy something important. Tammy wouldn't look at me. I looked back at the road, we were now halfway onto the bridge, and a large truck was coming at us. I think I screamed. There was nowhere to go. I remember being in a light gray space. I don't remember my feet and there was a tunnel to the right of me. Tammy was to the left of me. I knew what the tunnel was. I turned to Tammy, and I asked, "Are you staying, or are you going?" Tammy said, "I have to go back." I turned toward the tunnel and back at Tammy and she was gone. I woke up in the hospital. Everything hurts. I asked, "Where is Tammy?" They said she was a couple of doors down. I was grateful and relieved my daughter survived.

My Interpretation of the Events

I was still conversing with God when the truck hit. There was no pain, there was just, peace. My mother and I were surrounded by a breathtaking beautiful light filled with love. My mother was to my right and to my left were two beings. They were my size for my comfort yet they were vast. They were pure love, pure light. My mother did not seem to be paying attention to them or even hear them. I heard, "Little one, you have a choice. You can stay here with us or go back to earth to do what you went there to accomplish."

If I had known how difficult emotionally and physically painful life was going to be, I would have stayed with the Angels. I understood at that moment I had a mission bigger than myself. I said, "Send me back."

I looked at my mother, and she asked me, "Are you staying or are you going?"

I said, "I have to go back."

I was instantly aware of being so cold—so terribly cold, and voices.

My Story after the Accident

When I became conscious—what I remember and what I had been told:

I was told the first responder had put me to the side of the road and covered me with a blanket. They were waiting for the coroner to take me away. I had no vitals. As far as they were concerned I was deceased. My mother was trapped in the car and would be for a long time. At that moment she was the priority. They had to wait for the Jaws of Life (a tool to extricate victims from wrecks) to get her out of the vehicle.

Two related things happened simultaneously when the rescue squad came. I-74 runs right over I-55. My brother and his wife were headed west to Peoria to pick up something. It was a quick trip. When they drove onto the overpass on I-74 they saw all the rescue teams below them working on a horrific wreck. My brother and my beloved sister-in-law said, "God bless them and their family," not knowing they were praying for their own family. A couple of hours later, the police showed up at their door to tell them of the accident. My brother was stunned when he and his wife realized they had prayed for his mother and his sister.

My father could stand with support. When he heard the sirens, he rolled his wheelchair to the window and used the chair and the window sill to pull himself up so he could look out the window to see what was going on. My father told me later that he cried when he saw all the commotion at the end of the street. All the trees were bare; the bridge was within easy vision from the house. The details were not. In his tears, he said, "God bless them and their family." He did not know it was his wife and only daughter he was praying for.

Back to the Crash

"Do you know where you are?"

I remember wondering, "Why are these men cutting off my clothes? I just bought them and they're cutting off my favorite boots!"

"Tamara! Miss Dobbs! Do you know where you are?" They were so persistent. I said, "Gainesville, Georgia."

The men started laughing and crying at the same time. I don't know if it is true or not. I was told later that I was flat lined, and then I was talking, and that is why they were laughing with relief and joy. Apparently, I had graduated from high school with one member of the rescue team. This classmate was the one who refused to use the term <u>dead</u> when he found out who was under all the blood and the blanket. Head injuries are strange things. You would think the name of someone who was that important, would stay with me all my life. I have no memory of who he was or is. All I can say is thank you.

My injuries: a fractured knee, a shattered right hand, seventeen breaks in my ribs. One or more of those ribs punctured my left lung, and also fractured my skull. Some of my injuries would haunt me my entire life, others I would overcome besides all the hurdles to get well.

My next thought was, "Where is my Mother?" I began to ask for her. They informed me she was being taken care of and for me not to worry. She had a broken ankle, broken knee, broken pelvis, six broken ribs and her liver was bruised. The story was she made such a fuss and furiously fought with the rescue team. One of the team members said he wanted to knock her out to get her out of the car, for her own good. Of course he did not do that.

My Dad's Medication and Some Miracles

My dad's medication? A miracle happened. We had cats. Many cats. Mother had left the medications on the counter, close to the edge. One of the cats jumped up on the counter, landing directly on top of the medicine box. It slipped, startling the cat, She kicked the medicine box onto the floor, and all the pills exploded about the kitchen. When the neighbors came to tell my father that it was his wife and only daughter in the accident at the end of the road, he cried. These same people offered to help him in any way they could. When they stepped into the kitchen, they saw the mess of drugs on the floor and fixed his medicine properly. He was well taken care of while we were in the hospital.

Many miracles happened because of the accident. My life took a dramatic change over the next year, and years to come... A story for another time.

Mother was told she would never walk again. One month after leaving the hospital, she walked into her doctor's office. The doctor walked into the room we were waiting in and immediately turned around and left the room. He accused his staff of giving him the wrong chart. I was there when he came back into the room in disbelief. My mother said to him emphatically, "Never tell a patient that they will not heal! That they may not ever walk again! You do God an injustice! Miracles and perseverance happen." His apology was humble. She was using a walker and had a long way to go. Every day she worked at healing herself with the help of the "Power for Good," which was my mother's name for God.

HAVING A HISSY FIT

There were many Angelic or Holy Spirit moments over the next twenty plus years, and none of them involved near death or death experiences until one night I had a hissy fit. I am not a big drinker. I'll have a glass of wine or Margarita once in a while. Forgetting my capacity, one evening I had a few too many beers. I don't like beer, and someone triggered my anger. I got angry enough to drink an entire bottle of Rum. I stupidly ended up with alcohol poisoning. In this case, long story short, in the emergency room my heart stopped twice. There were no lights, no tunnel, just a soft amused voice saying, *"You think you're coming home now?"* Laughter sounding, like tinkling bells. *"You are right where we want you. You have to finish your mission."* I was so miserable for at least a week. A week where I was humbled—a week that I grew in my compassion for others—a week that I realized I had lost my way.

God was about to show me my path.

MANY ROOMS

Two months later, I woke up screaming that I was having a heart attack and an 800 lb. gorilla was hugging me! For two years, I had been telling the medical profession I was having heart attacks. The doctors would do an EKG and send me home. They thought I was having panic attacks or a fibromyalgia attack. The night I had the hissy fit started with a discussion about the drug dealers in our area, and then how I was being melodramatic, and my insistent claim that I was sick. I'm not sure how eight doctors and five hospital visits could miss that my gallbladder had grown to the size of a baseball, and when it was removed, it was five pounds and filled with pus and stones. I was dying, and they said I was a hypochondriac. My mate was tired of hearing that I was sick, and he had begun to believe them. I was in the hospital two days before they diagnosed the issue. When they finally found the cause, they couldn't take the gallbladder out until the infection was under control.

When the gallbladder was finally removed, it was discovered that my body was filled with the leakage of the rotten organ. The hospital's staff, in its infinite wisdom, thought that it was just fine to send me home with a 101.5 temperature. I was not to call them unless it hit 103. Even when I went in to see the surgeon to remove the drainage tube, I had a temperature over 101. He was not concerned. I was told I needed to walk more and drink more water.

About a week after I was out of the hospital, I died. This was not a confirmed death as far as the medical profession is concerned, but I died. I'll start with Steve's story the way I think he might tell it. If you ever meet him, ask him about it. (I just wonder if his story will change with me not around.)

Steve's Story

Tamara and I share a California king size bed. She cocoons in blankets no matter what time of year it is, and it is late May in Florida. She sleeps at one end, and I sleep under the fan with a sheet. We have this beautiful half Maine Coon black cat. His name is Gogi. He is very in tune with his human mother. Tamara had been miserable on this particular night; we went to bed early. An hour or so later, Gogi, who doesn't know how to meow, squeaks, and he weighs about 18 pounds. He starts pouncing on me, heavy and squeaking in desperation. He absolutely got my attention. I started calling out to Tamara. "Tam! Something is wrong with Gogi!" She did not respond. Gogi moved to the other end of the bed and started pouncing on Tamara. I knew without a doubt that something wasn't right. Tamara was sleeping on her side and almost on her stomach. I touched her and still no response. I started yelling. Still, there was no response. Flipping her over, I listened for a heartbeat, I heard nothing; she was not breathing. I have never punched a woman in my life, and I punched her twice: once in the heart and once in the diaphragm. Then I started shaking her. She responded. I held her, and we cried. She kept asking me why I didn't let her go.

I WALKED WITH JESUS

My Story

I have had a lot of friends and family pass. Some years, you would have thought I lived in a war zone. In one year, seventeen friends and family members died. The largest chapter in this book is about losing loved ones. Most people who have read this book, have told me the chapter on "Death and Healing" has given them peace. And that is why I have to share where I was when Gogi and Steve fought to bring me back.

To those who read the Bible, I do too. After the head injuries, I could no longer quote the Bible, or any of the great religious books. I have read most of the major ones, and I remember enough to get my point across. Remember the part where Jesus says, "I go before you to prepare many mansions." There is so much more to heaven or the afterlife than we can even imagine.

A man came to me that night. The color of his skin was mocha; he had mahogany-colored curly hair, and his eyes: the kindest eyes I have ever seen, green, brown, gray and blue, and they shifted colors. He offered me his hand. I can still feel his touch. I can still hear his voice. I can still see what he was showing me. Jesus and I journeyed the heavens. When we speak, I call Him Yeshua.

I closed my eyes before typing any more of this story. I had to breathe it in. Sometimes, I feel as if I am still there. I can feel His presence.

What I saw, what I felt, what I knew at the time so filled my senses that I never wanted to come back. The colors, the music, the singing, the joy and love was so enveloping, so beautiful that it cannot be described in human terms. And there are amazing rooms (mansions?) filled with joyous souls! Yeshua said to me, "There is a place for all of you, all beliefs. God is love and *you* are loved." Then I was in Steve's arms with a cat standing on his hind legs sniffing my nose.

This little book had already been written and in the publisher's hands when the last two events happened. I received a call to have *Prayer When You Don't Have the Words* taken over by a broker. They asked me to add twenty pages, change a few things, and get it to them as soon as possible. I have been slow to respond. When I was asked to add twenty pages, I thought, "Okay, I will add a few prayers. Then I was stumped. I couldn't write. Nothing worked. I forgot to do something so small, so easy—I forgot to walk my talk. In my frustration, I found myself on my knees asking God for help. I gave thanks for God and my Angels. Then I asked for more humor in my life. I had been diagnosed with Lymes disease, and life had gotten just too serious. Within the hour, I was told a very stupid funny joke. It still makes me laugh. I asked for inspiration, and Steve asked me to go to one of his monotonous early morning meetings. I growled and altered my schedule by fifteen minutes so I could help him out. The subject matter of the day was *inspiration.* The third thing I asked for was subject matter. I was told a second joke, and that joke made me relive my walk with Yeshua. I now had the subject matter. The fourth thing I asked for was time and energy to write. God gave Steve a second job, and it started the very next day. I wrote over five thousand words in four and a half hours.

Other blessings that came from that prayer: My neighbor, unbeknownst to me, had been an editor for two famous magazines. One of my best friends is also an editor and she has written several award winning historical romance novels. A new friend of mine is a famous artist. He and his wife offered me any painting I wanted for my new book cover. A wonderful, gifted young lady came into my life who was willing to trade massages for photos.

Tamara Michelle Dobbs

This is how I came to believe!
The Holy Spirit… also known as Angels.
And Yeshua, also known as… Jesus.
I pray this little book inspires you to have hope,
helps you with your losses and
helps you with your wins!
May this little book help you find the words.

<u>GOD BLESS!</u>

Website: www.tamaradobbslife.com

www.ingramcontent.com/pod-product-compliance
Lightning Source LLC
Chambersburg PA
CBHW061747070526
44585CB00025B/2820